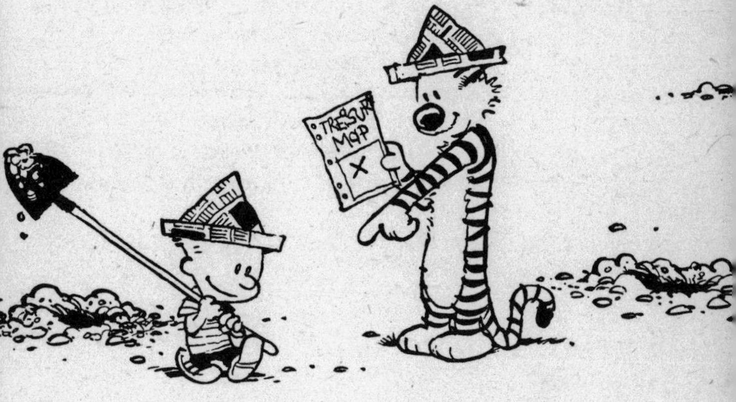
TREASUR
MAP
X

*Also by Bill Watterson:*

CALVIN AND HOBBES
SOMETHING UNDER THE BED IS DROOLING
YUKON HO!
WEIRDOS FROM ANOTHER PLANET
LAZY SUNDAY BOOK
REVENGE OF THE BABY-SAT
THE AUTHORITATIVE CALVIN AND HOBBES
SCIENTIFIC PROGRESS GOES 'BOINK'
ATTACK OF THE DERANGED MUTANT KILLER MONSTER SNOW GOONS
THE INDISPENSABLE CALVIN AND HOBBES
THE DAYS ARE JUST PACKED

*Taken from* CALVIN AND HOBBES:
CALVIN AND HOBBES 1: THEREBY HANGS A TALE
CALVIN AND HOBBES 2: ONE DAY THE WIND WILL CHANGE

# Calvin and Hobbes

## 3: IN THE SHADOW OF THE NIGHT

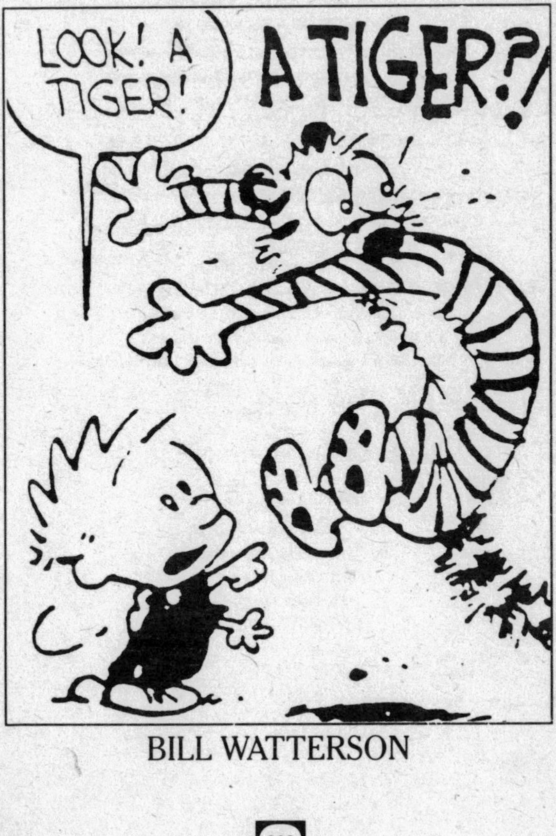
LOOK! A TIGER!
A TIGER?!

BILL WATTERSON

WARNER BOOKS

A *Warner* Book

First published in Great Britain in 1992
by Warner Books
Reprinted 1993, 1994, 1995

Copyright © 1987, 1992 by Bill Watterson,
distributed by Universal Press Syndicate
Calvin and Hobbes© is syndicated internationally by
Universal Press Syndicate

The contents of this edition were first published as part
of *Calvin and Hobbes* © 1987 by Bill Watterson, published by
Sphere Books 1988

ISBN 0 7515 0510 2

Printed in England by Clays Ltd, St Ives plc

Warner Books
A Division of
Little, Brown and Company (UK)
Brettenham House
Lancaster Place
London WC2E 7EN

TO MELISSA

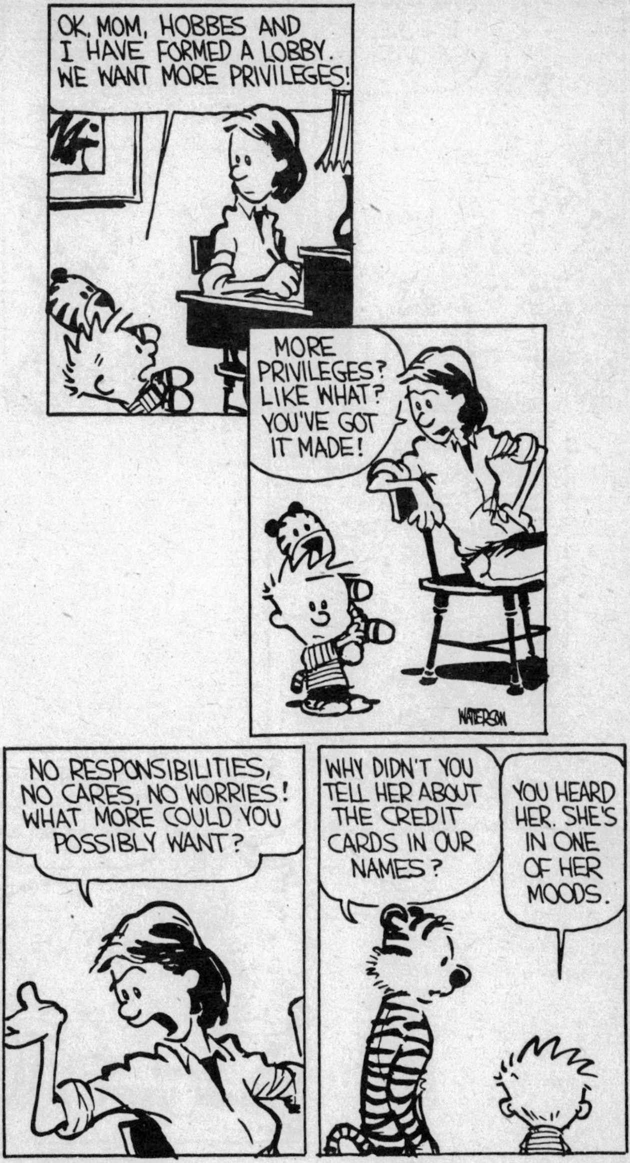
OK, MOM, HOBBES AND I HAVE FORMED A LOBBY. WE WANT MORE PRIVILEGES!
MORE PRIVILEGES? LIKE WHAT? YOU'VE GOT IT MADE!
WATERSON
NO RESPONSIBILITIES, NO CARES, NO WORRIES! WHAT MORE COULD YOU POSSIBLY WANT?
WHY DIDN'T YOU TELL HER ABOUT THE CREDIT CARDS IN OUR NAMES?
YOU HEARD HER. SHE'S IN ONE OF HER MOODS.

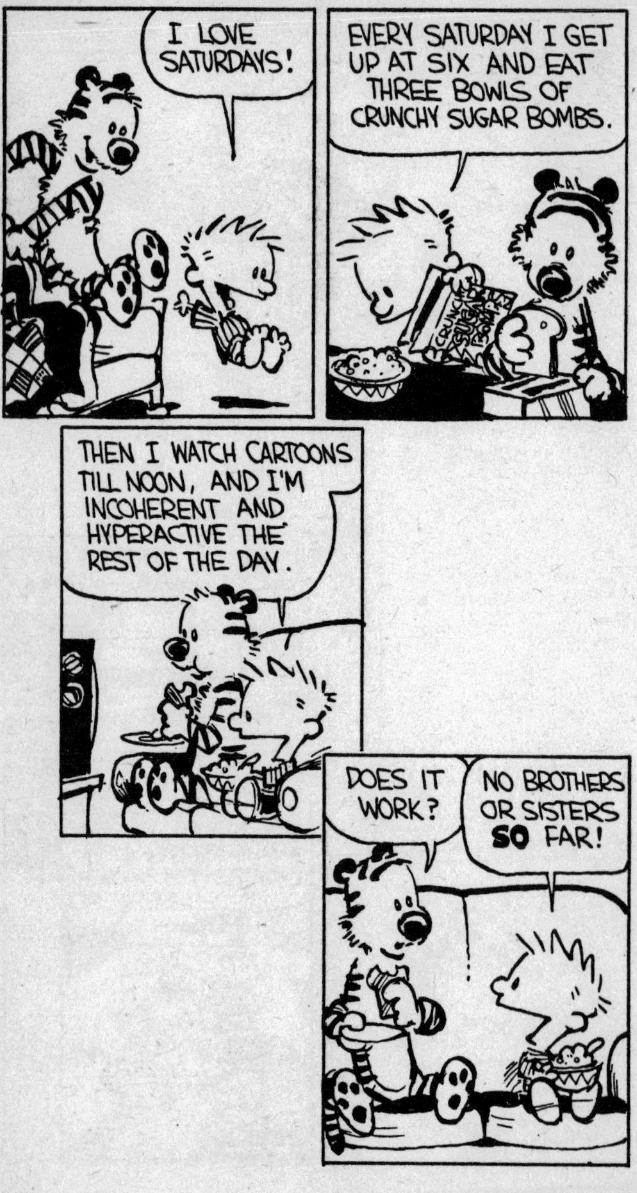
I LOVE SATURDAYS!
EVERY SATURDAY I GET UP AT SIX AND EAT THREE BOWLS OF CRUNCHY SUGAR BOMBS.
CRUNCHY SUGAR BOMBS
THEN I WATCH CARTOONS TILL NOON, AND I'M INCOHERENT AND HYPERACTIVE THE REST OF THE DAY.
DOES IT WORK?
NO BROTHERS OR SISTERS **SO** FAR!

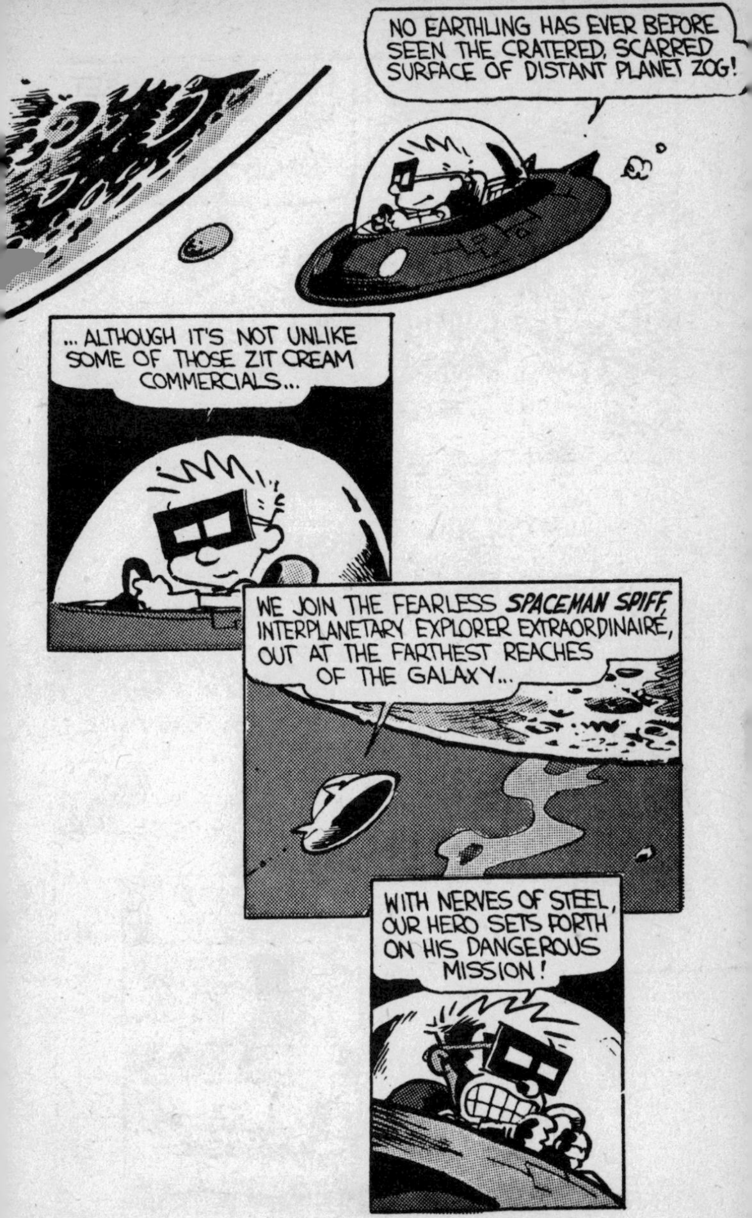
WE JOIN THE FEARLESS SPACEMAN SPIFF, INTERPLANETARY EXPLORER EXTRAORDINAIRE, OUT AT THE FARTHEST REACHES OF THE GALAXY...
WITH NERVES OF STEEL, OUR HERO SETS FORTH ON HIS DANGEROUS MISSION!
NO EARTHLING HAS EVER BEFORE SEEN THE CRATERED, SCARRED SURFACE OF DISTANT PLANET ZOG!
... ALTHOUGH IT'S NOT UNLIKE SOME OF THOSE ZIT CREAM COMMERCIALS...

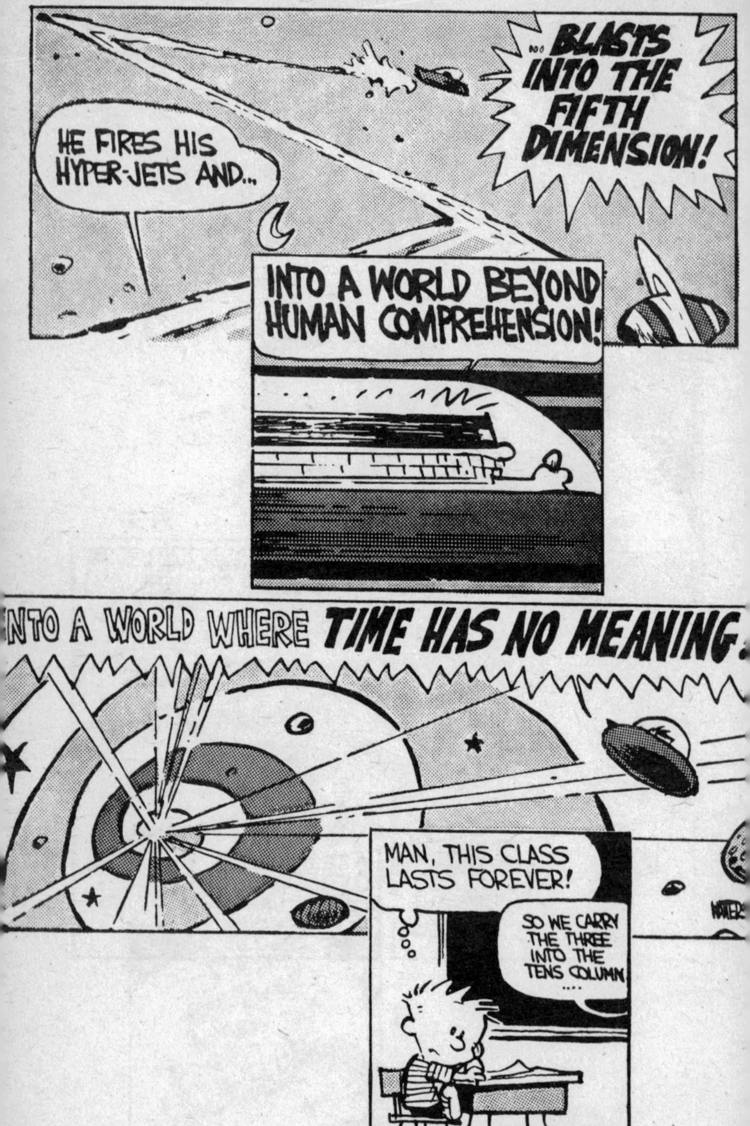
HE FIRES HIS HYPER-JETS AND...
...BLASTS INTO THE FIFTH DIMENSION!
INTO A WORLD BEYOND HUMAN COMPREHENSION!
INTO A WORLD WHERE TIME HAS NO MEANING.
MAN, THIS CLASS LASTS FOREVER!
SO WE CARRY THE THREE INTO THE TENS COLUMN....

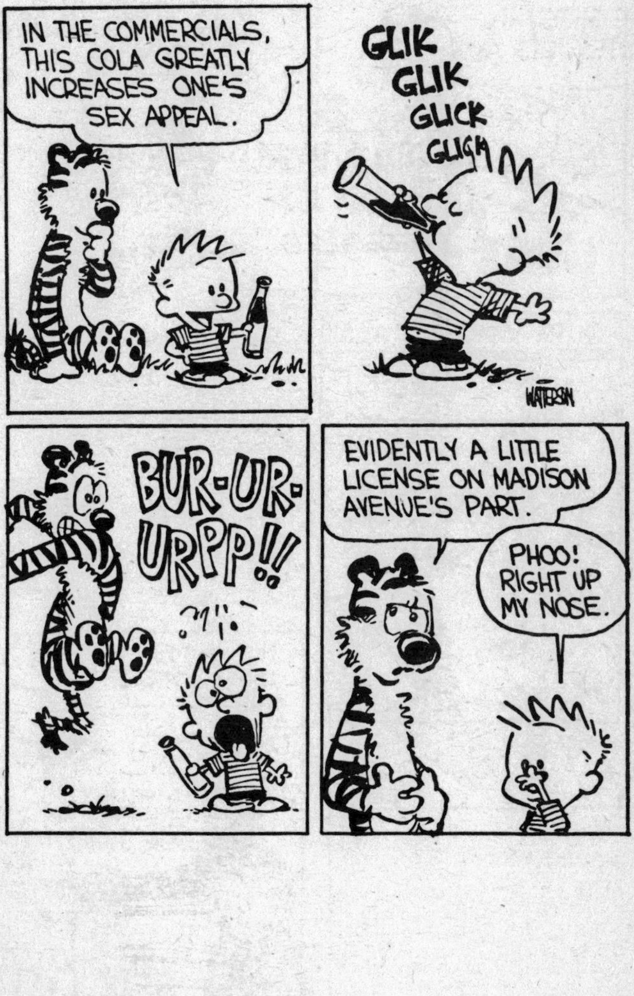
IN THE COMMERCIALS, THIS COLA GREATLY INCREASES ONE'S SEX APPEAL.
GLIK GLIK GLICK GLIGH
WATERSON
BUR-UR-URPP!!
EVIDENTLY A LITTLE LICENSE ON MADISON AVENUE'S PART.
PHOO! RIGHT UP MY NOSE.

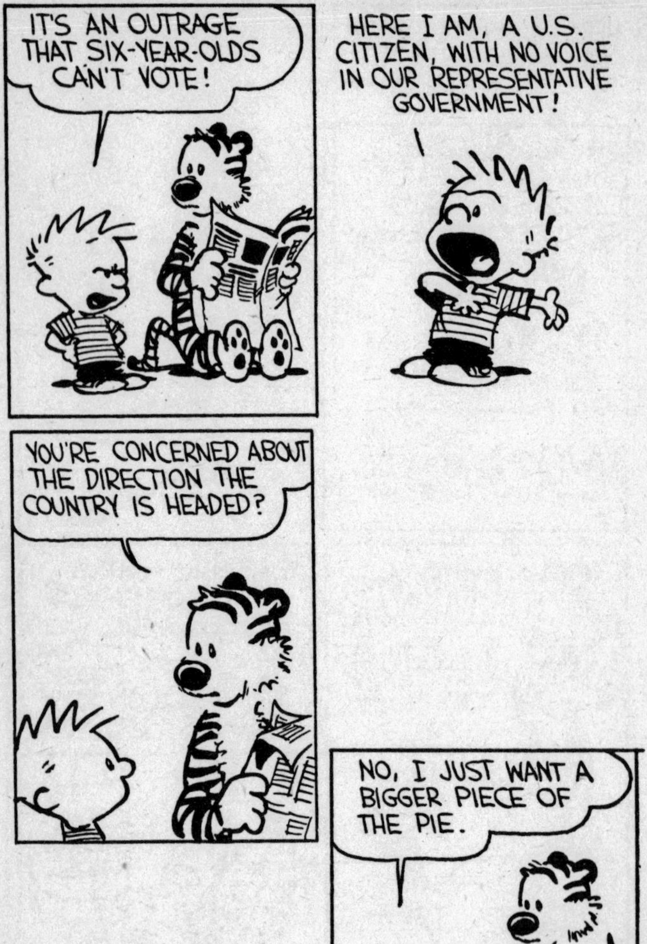
IT'S AN OUTRAGE THAT SIX-YEAR-OLDS CAN'T VOTE!
HERE I AM, A U.S. CITIZEN, WITH NO VOICE IN OUR REPRESENTATIVE GOVERNMENT!
YOU'RE CONCERNED ABOUT THE DIRECTION THE COUNTRY IS HEADED?
NO, I JUST WANT A BIGGER PIECE OF THE PIE.
WATERSON

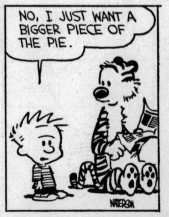

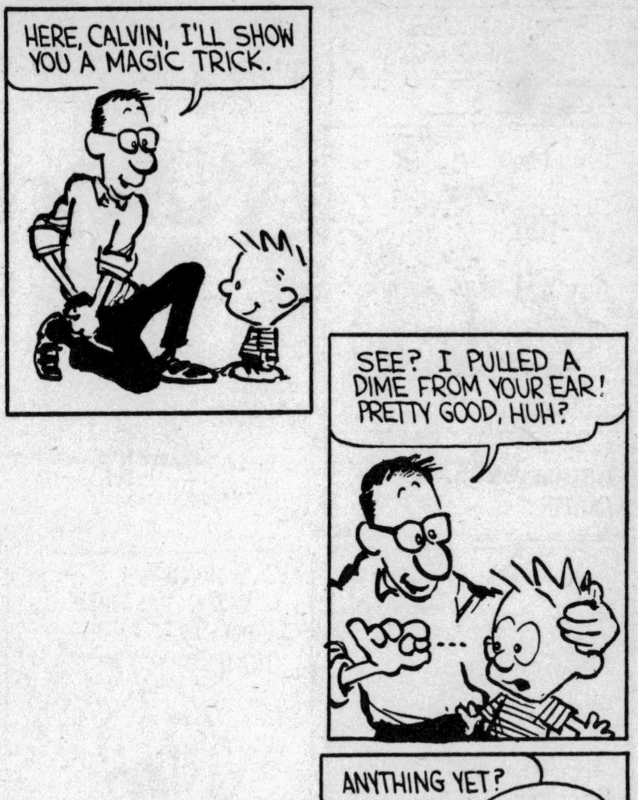
HERE, CALVIN, I'LL SHOW YOU A MAGIC TRICK.
SEE? I PULLED A DIME FROM YOUR EAR! PRETTY GOOD, HUH?
ANYTHING YET?
J-JUST A B-B-BLOODY N-NOSE.

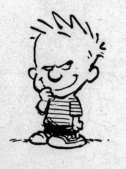

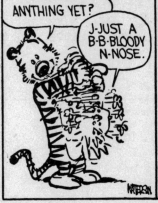

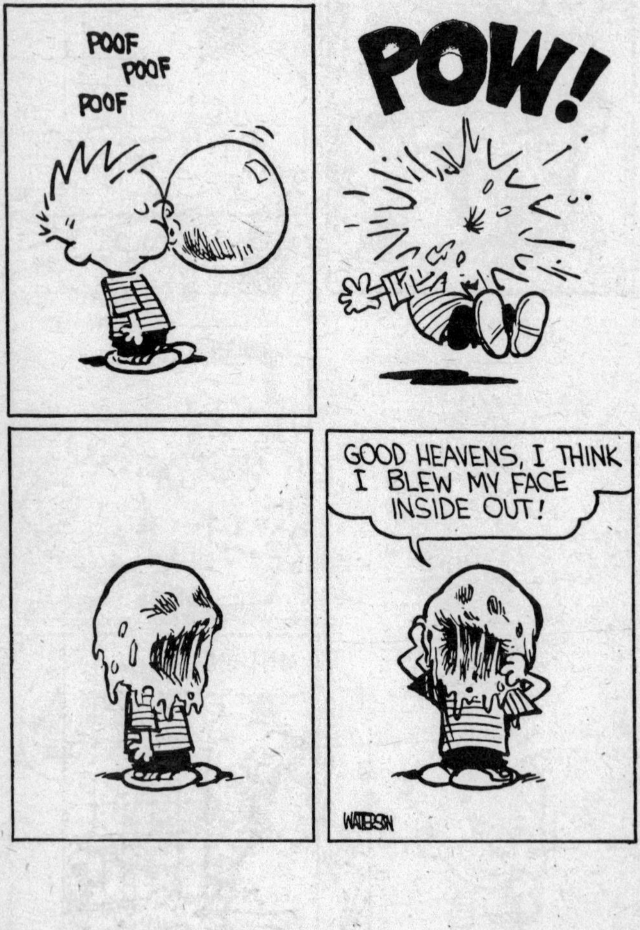
POOF
POOF
POOF
POW!
GOOD HEAVENS, I THINK I BLEW MY FACE INSIDE OUT!
WATTERSON

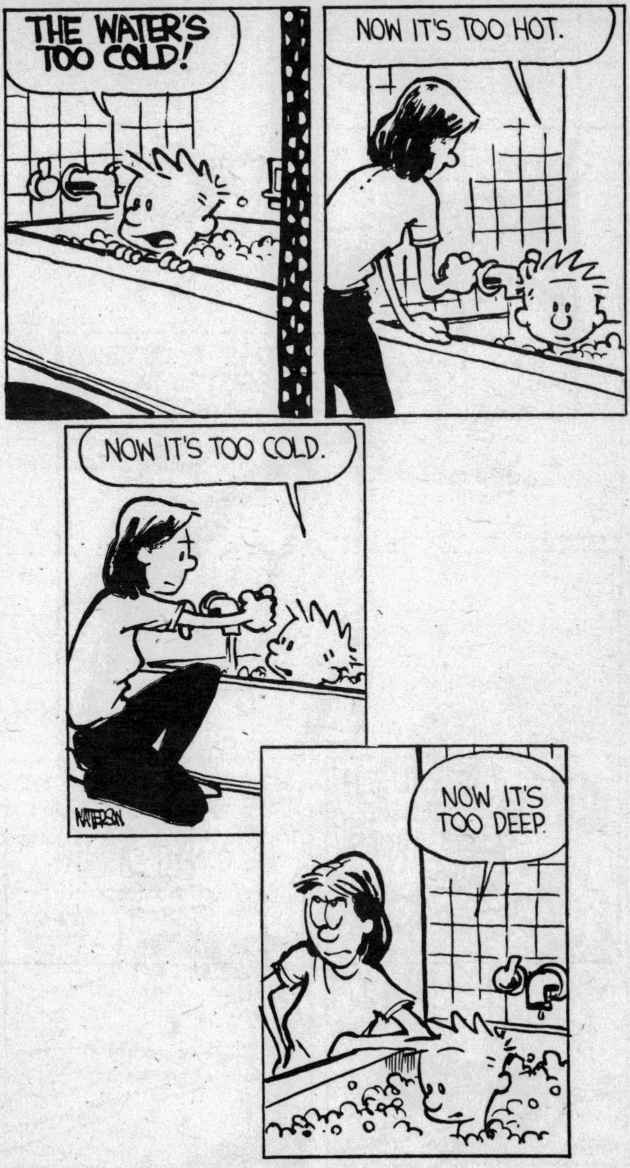
THE WATER'S TOO COLD!
NOW IT'S TOO HOT.
NOW IT'S TOO COLD.
NOW IT'S TOO DEEP.

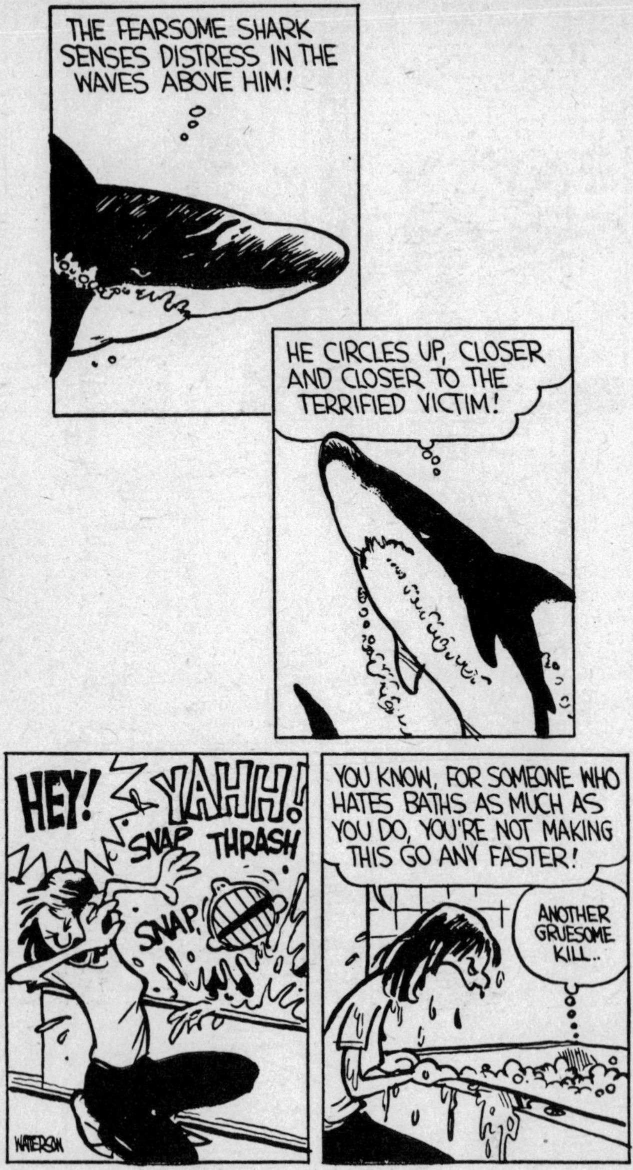
THE FEARSOME SHARK SENSES DISTRESS IN THE WAVES ABOVE HIM!
HE CIRCLES UP, CLOSER AND CLOSER TO THE TERRIFIED VICTIM!
HEY!
YAHH!
SNAP
THRASH
SNAP
WATERSON
YOU KNOW, FOR SOMEONE WHO HATES BATHS AS MUCH AS YOU DO, YOU'RE NOT MAKING THIS GO ANY FASTER!
ANOTHER GRUESOME KILL..

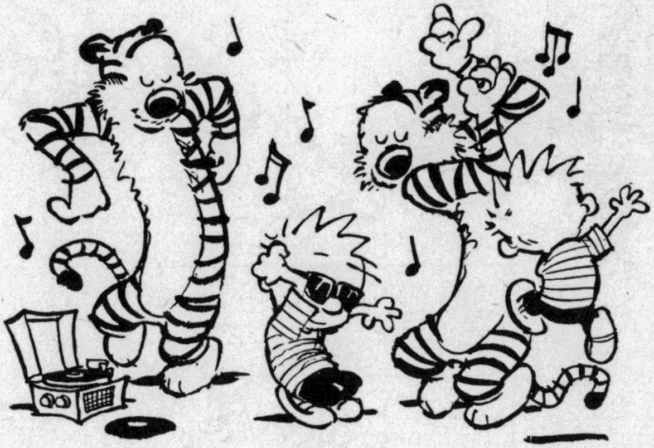

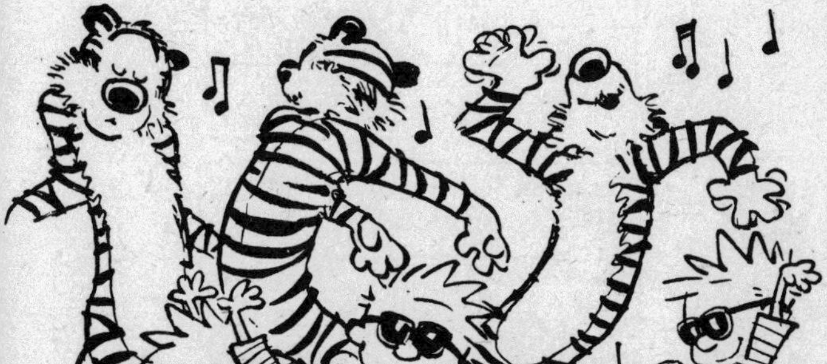

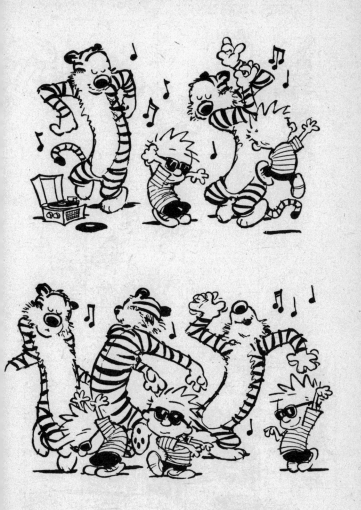

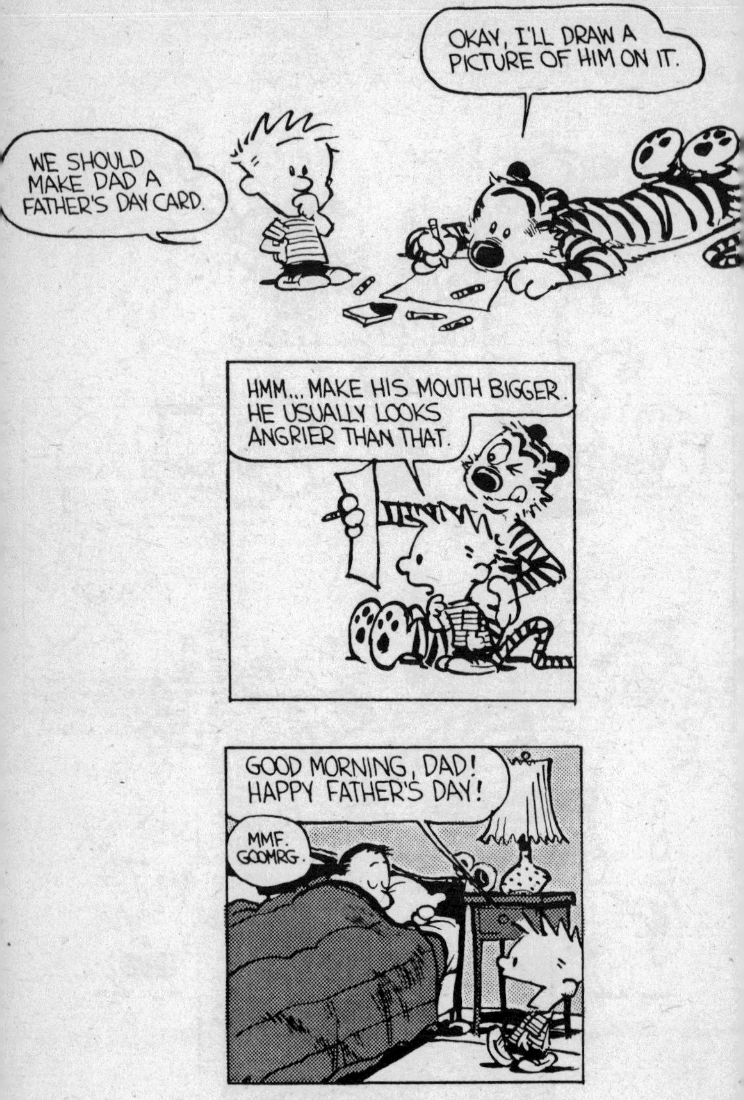
WE SHOULD MAKE DAD A FATHER'S DAY CARD.
OKAY, I'LL DRAW A PICTURE OF HIM ON IT.
HMM... MAKE HIS MOUTH BIGGER. HE USUALLY LOOKS ANGRIER THAN THAT.
GOOD MORNING, DAD! HAPPY FATHER'S DAY!
MMF. GOOMRG.

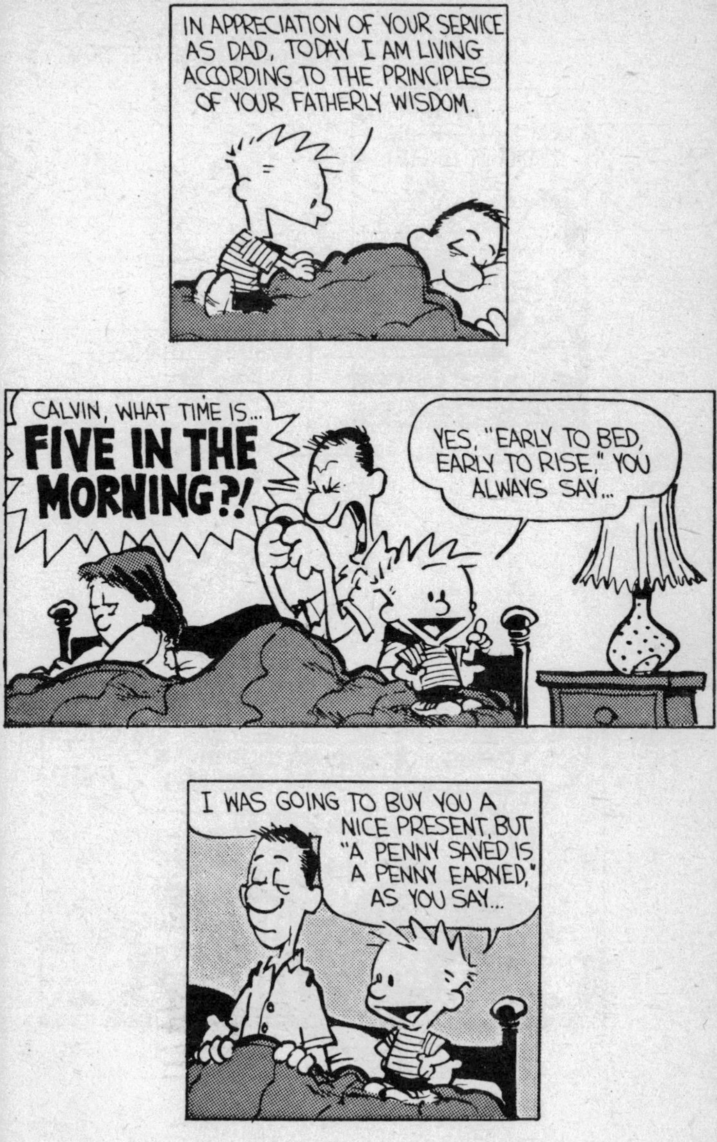
IN APPRECIATION OF YOUR SERVICE AS DAD, TODAY I AM LIVING ACCORDING TO THE PRINCIPLES OF YOUR FATHERLY WISDOM.
CALVIN, WHAT TIME IS... FIVE IN THE MORNING?!
YES, "EARLY TO BED, EARLY TO RISE," YOU ALWAYS SAY...
I WAS GOING TO BUY YOU A NICE PRESENT, BUT "A PENNY SAVED IS A PENNY EARNED," AS YOU SAY...

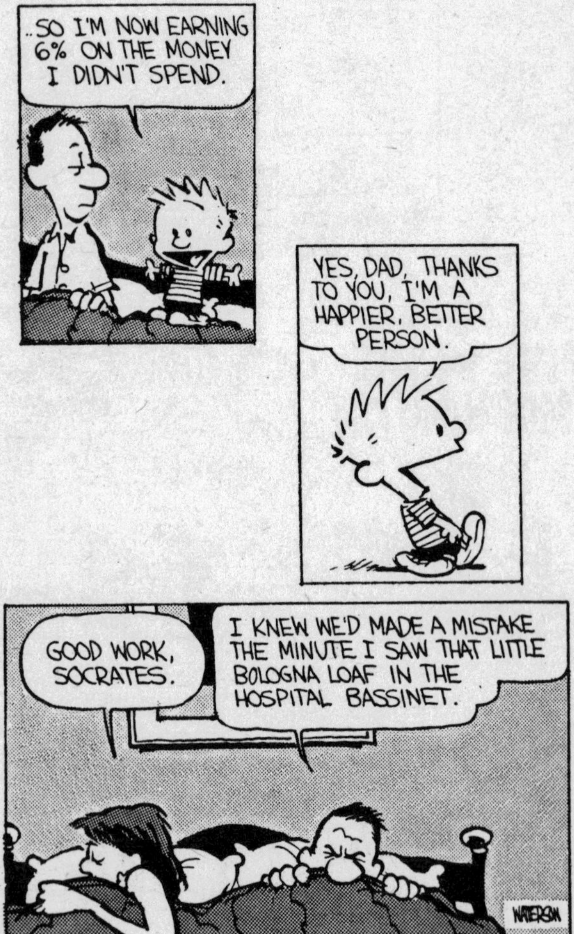
..SO I'M NOW EARNING 6% ON THE MONEY I DIDN'T SPEND.
YES, DAD, THANKS TO YOU, I'M A HAPPIER, BETTER PERSON.
GOOD WORK, SOCRATES.
I KNEW WE'D MADE A MISTAKE THE MINUTE I SAW THAT LITTLE BOLOGNA LOAF IN THE HOSPITAL BASSINET.
WATERSON

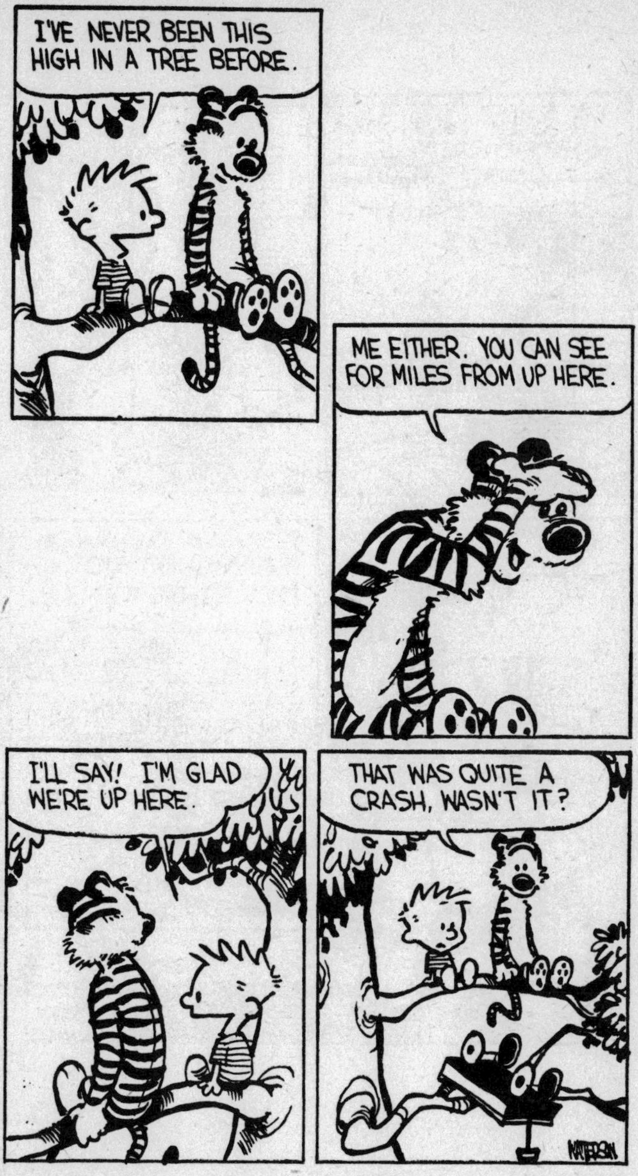

I'VE NEVER BEEN THIS HIGH IN A TREE BEFORE.
ME EITHER. YOU CAN SEE FOR MILES FROM UP HERE.
I'LL SAY! I'M GLAD WE'RE UP HERE.
THAT WAS QUITE A CRASH, WASN'T IT?
WATTERSON

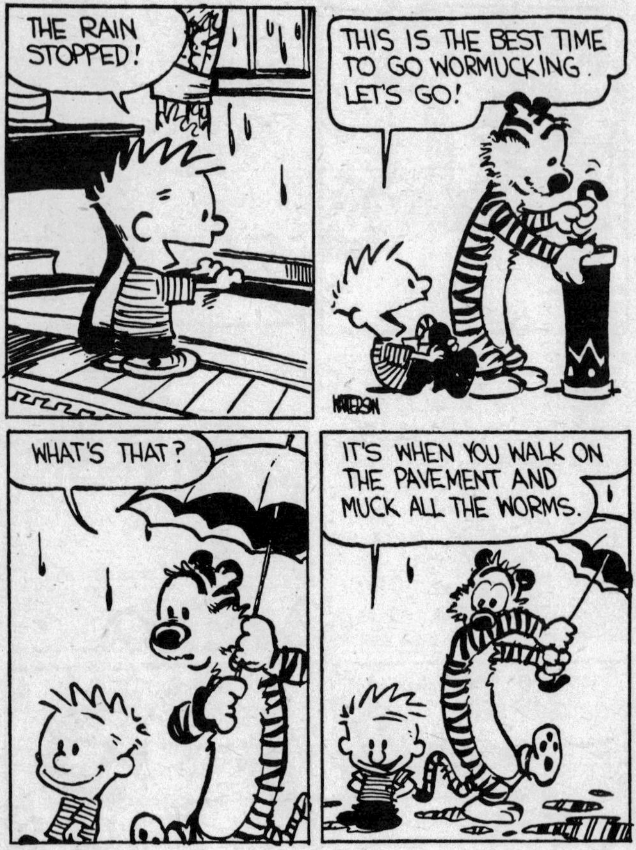
THE RAIN STOPPED!
THIS IS THE BEST TIME TO GO WORMUCKING. LET'S GO!
WATTERSON
WHAT'S THAT?
IT'S WHEN YOU WALK ON THE PAVEMENT AND MUCK ALL THE WORMS.

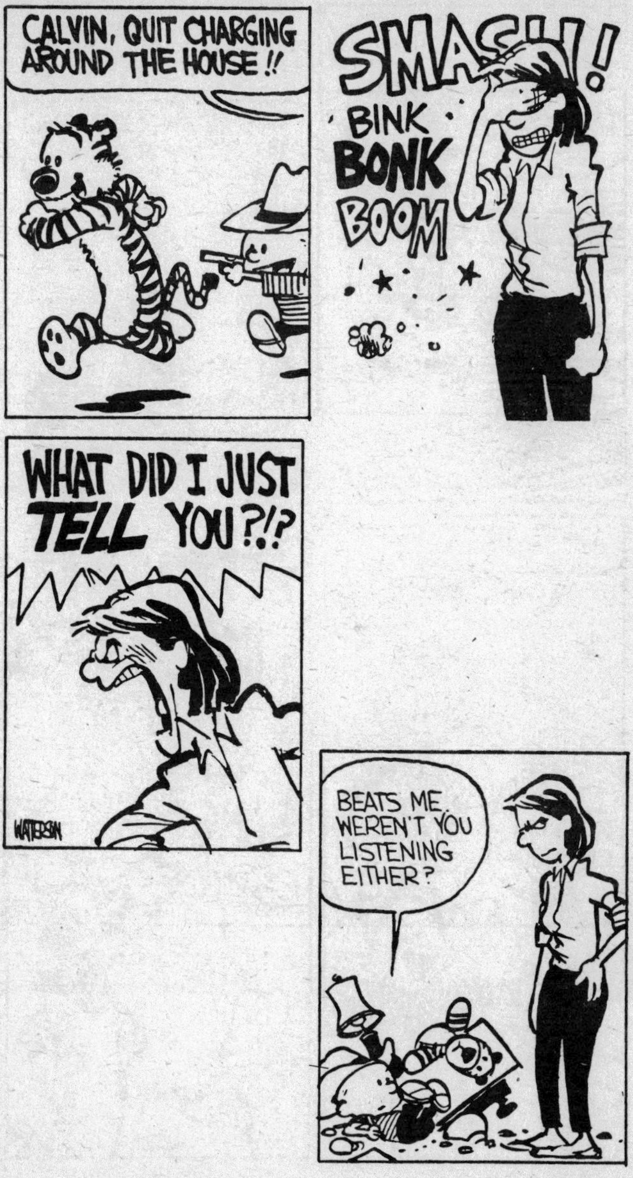
CALVIN, QUIT CHARGING AROUND THE HOUSE !!
SMASH!
BINK
BONK
BOOM
WHAT DID I JUST TELL YOU ?!?
WATTERSON
BEATS ME. WEREN'T YOU LISTENING EITHER?

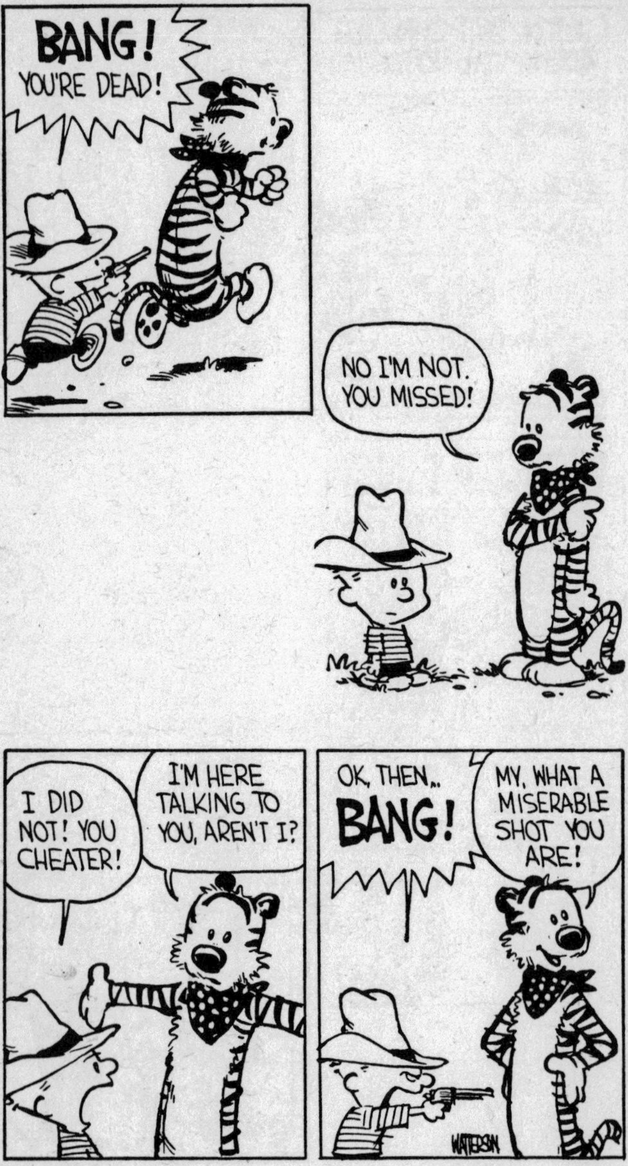
BANG! YOU'RE DEAD!
NO I'M NOT. YOU MISSED!
I DID NOT! YOU CHEATER!
I'M HERE TALKING TO YOU, AREN'T I?
OK, THEN.. BANG!
MY, WHAT A MISERABLE SHOT YOU ARE!

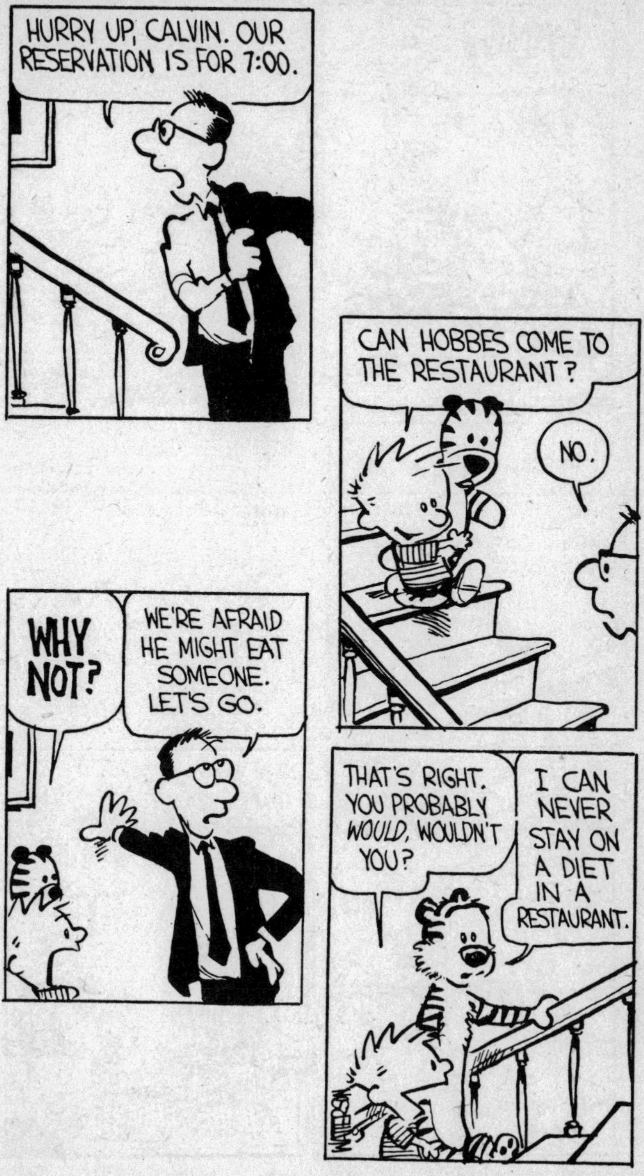
HURRY UP, CALVIN. OUR RESERVATION IS FOR 7:00.
CAN HOBBES COME TO THE RESTAURANT?
NO.
WHY NOT?
WE'RE AFRAID HE MIGHT EAT SOMEONE. LET'S GO.
THAT'S RIGHT. YOU PROBABLY *WOULD*, WOULDN'T YOU?
I CAN NEVER STAY ON A DIET IN A RESTAURANT.

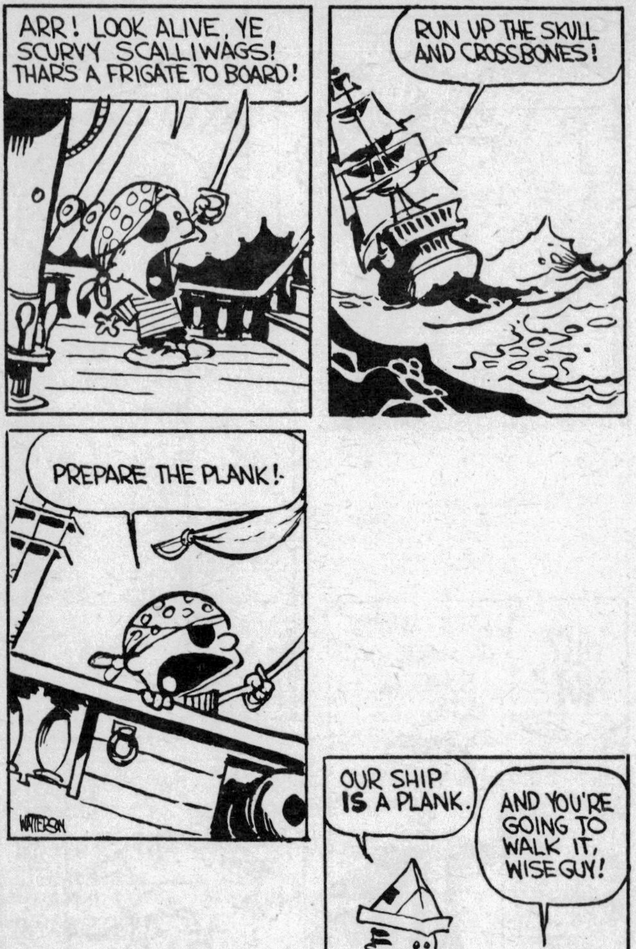
ARR! LOOK ALIVE, YE SCURVY SCALLIWAGS! THAR'S A FRIGATE TO BOARD!
RUN UP THE SKULL AND CROSSBONES!
PREPARE THE PLANK!
OUR SHIP **IS** A PLANK.
AND YOU'RE GOING TO WALK IT, WISE GUY!

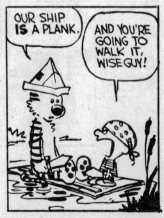

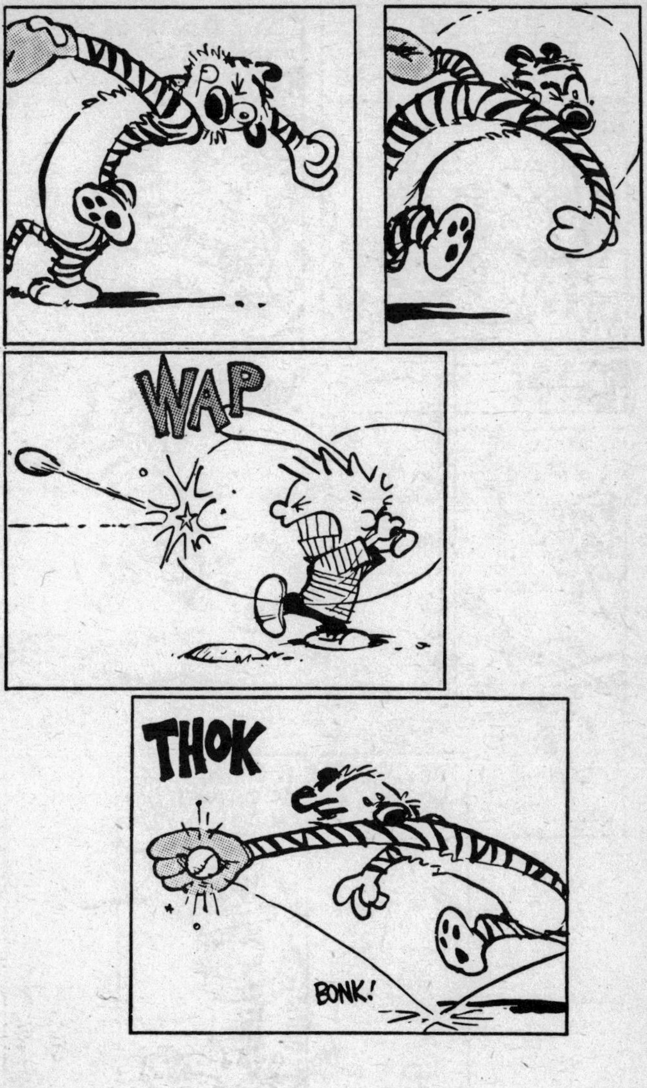
WAP
THOK
BONK!

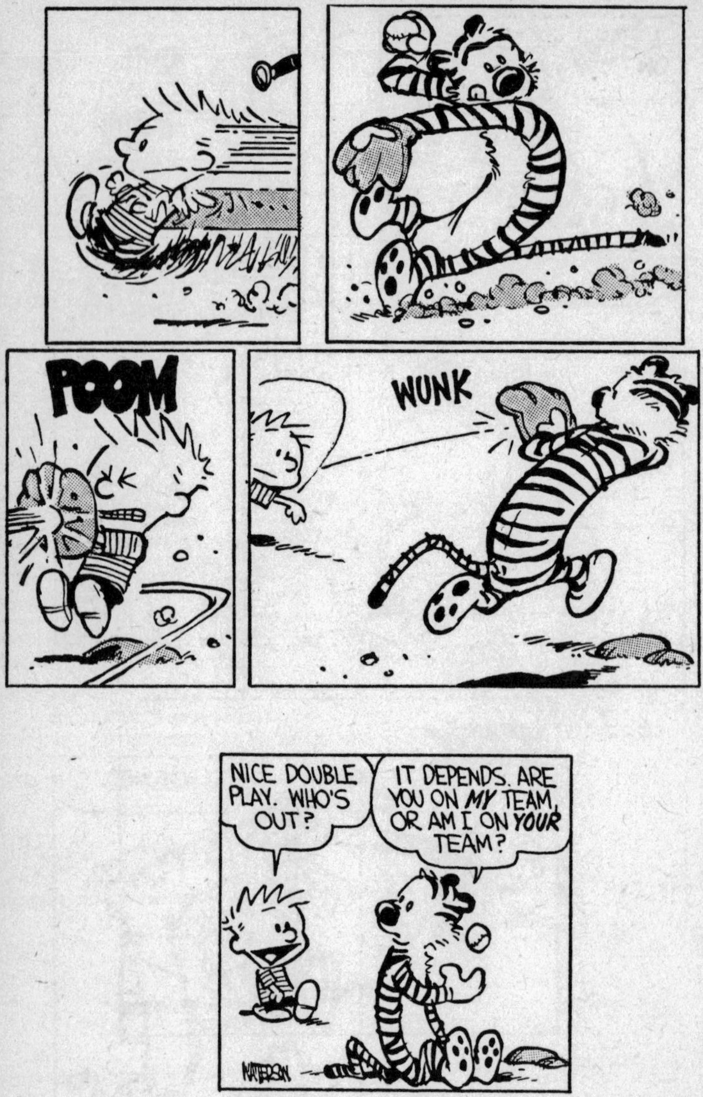

POOM
WUNK
NICE DOUBLE PLAY. WHO'S OUT?
IT DEPENDS. ARE YOU ON *MY* TEAM, OR AM I ON *YOUR* TEAM?
WATTERSON

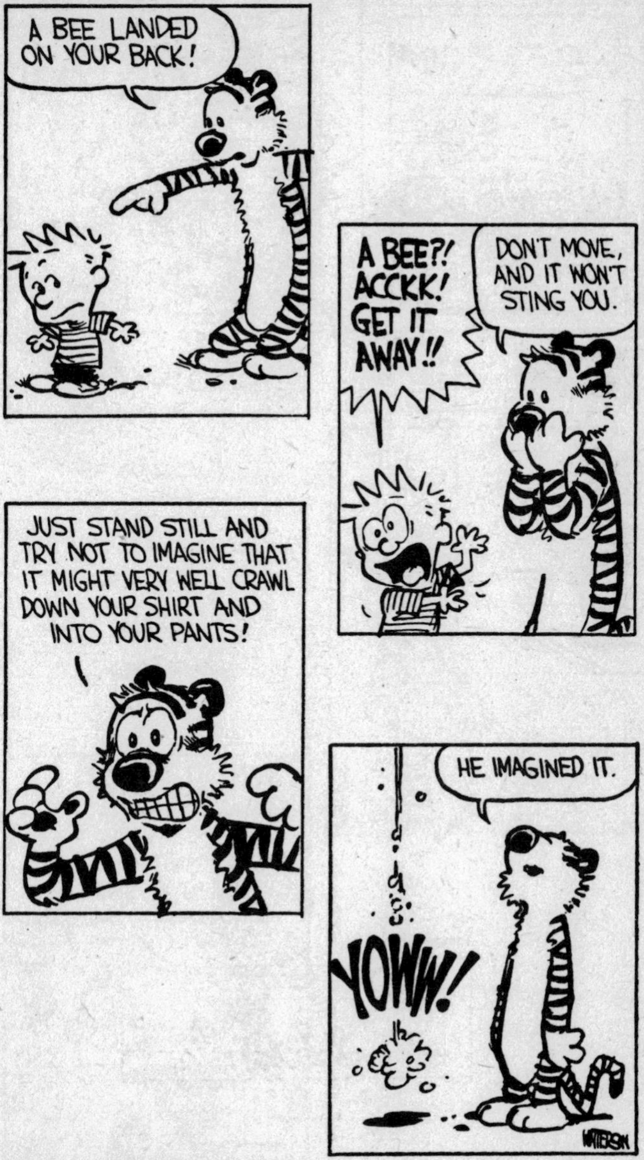
A BEE LANDED ON YOUR BACK!
A BEE?! ACCKK! GET IT AWAY!!
DON'T MOVE, AND IT WON'T STING YOU.
JUST STAND STILL AND TRY NOT TO IMAGINE THAT IT MIGHT VERY WELL CRAWL DOWN YOUR SHIRT AND INTO YOUR PANTS!
YOWW!
HE IMAGINED IT.

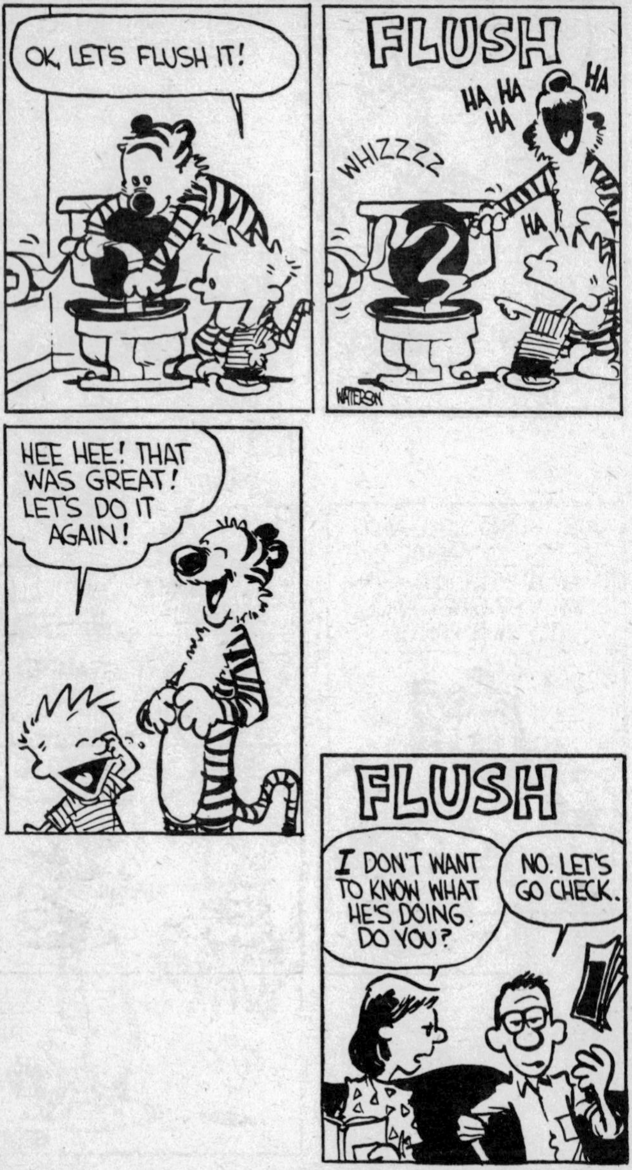
OK, LET'S FLUSH IT!
FLUSH
HA HA HA
HA
WHIZZZZ
HA
WATTERSON
HEE HEE! THAT WAS GREAT! LET'S DO IT AGAIN!
FLUSH
I DON'T WANT TO KNOW WHAT HE'S DOING. DO YOU?
NO. LET'S GO CHECK.

I'VE HAD TROUBLE CHOOSING A NEW HOBBY.
FIRST I WANTED TO COLLECT BUGS.
THEN I WANTED TO COLLECT STAMPS.
WHAT DID YOU DECIDE ON?
STAMPED BUGS.

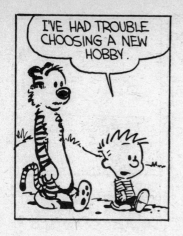

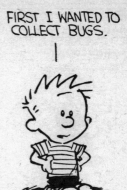

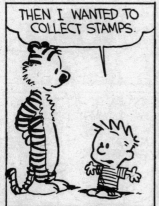

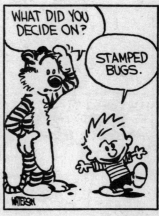

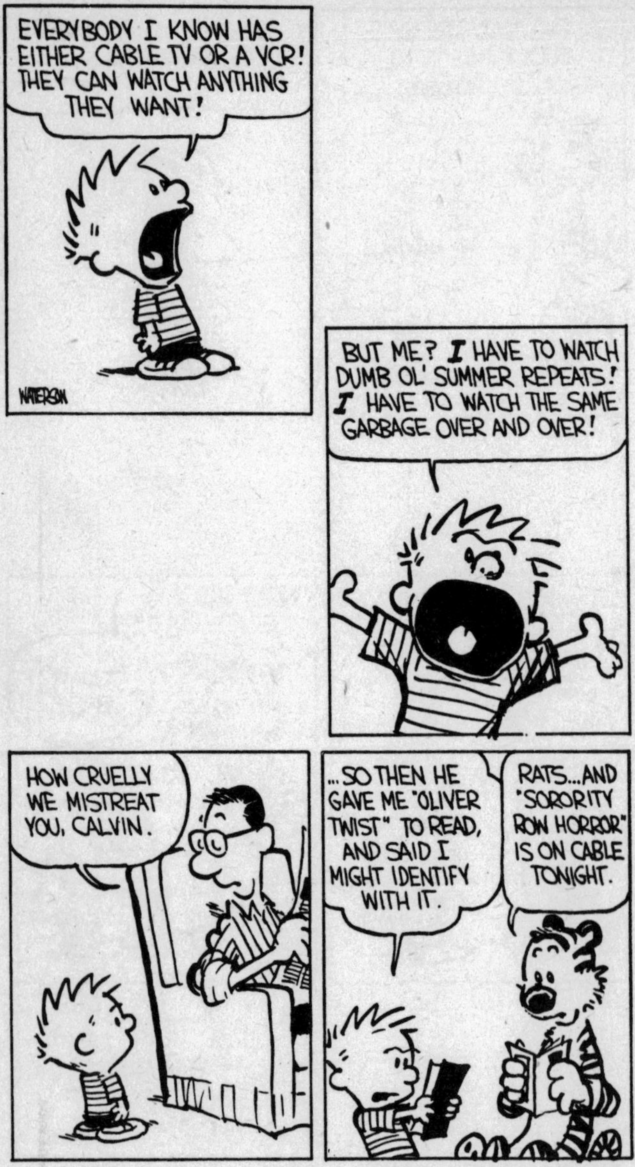
EVERYBODY I KNOW HAS EITHER CABLE TV OR A VCR! THEY CAN WATCH ANYTHING THEY WANT!
WATERSON
BUT ME? I HAVE TO WATCH DUMB OL' SUMMER REPEATS! I HAVE TO WATCH THE SAME GARBAGE OVER AND OVER!
HOW CRUELLY WE MISTREAT YOU, CALVIN.
...SO THEN HE GAVE ME "OLIVER TWIST" TO READ, AND SAID I MIGHT IDENTIFY WITH IT.
RATS...AND "SORORITY ROW HORROR" IS ON CABLE TONIGHT.

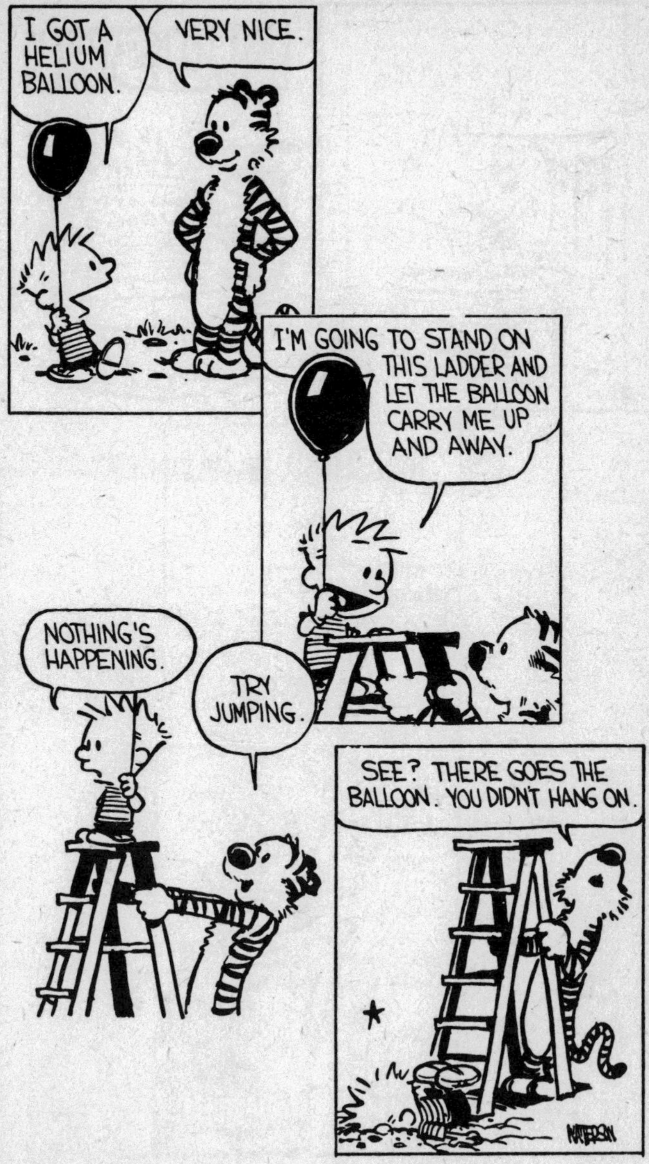
I GOT A HELIUM BALLOON.
VERY NICE.
I'M GOING TO STAND ON THIS LADDER AND LET THE BALLOON CARRY ME UP AND AWAY.
NOTHING'S HAPPENING.
TRY JUMPING.
SEE? THERE GOES THE BALLOON. YOU DIDN'T HANG ON.
WATTERSON

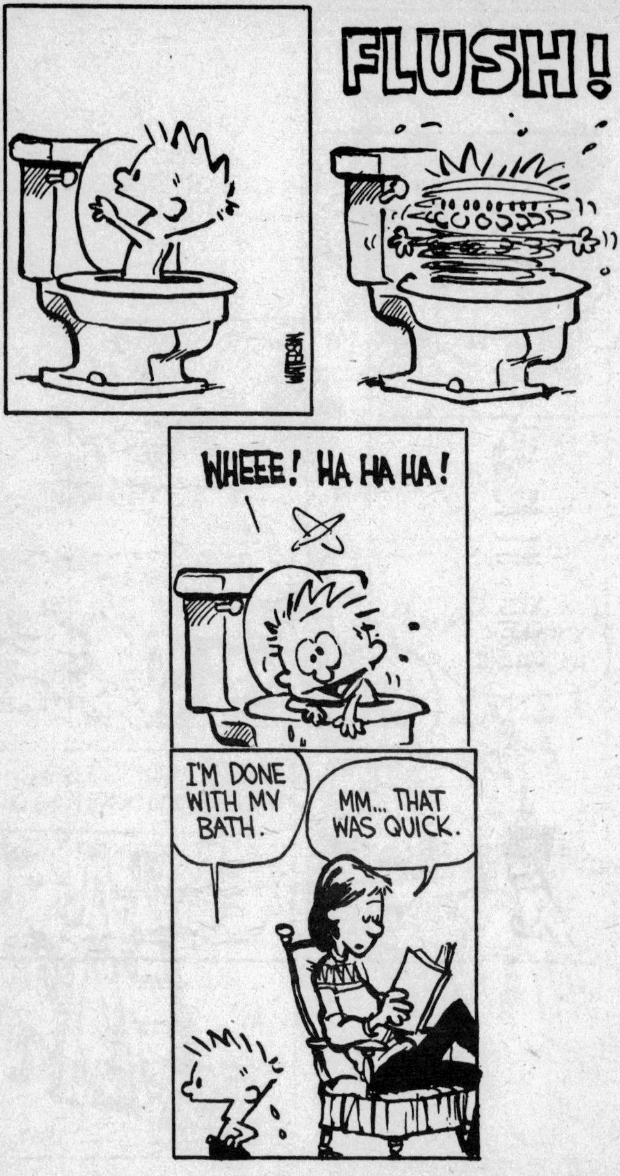

FLUSH!
WHEEE! HA HA HA!
I'M DONE WITH MY BATH.
MM... THAT WAS QUICK.

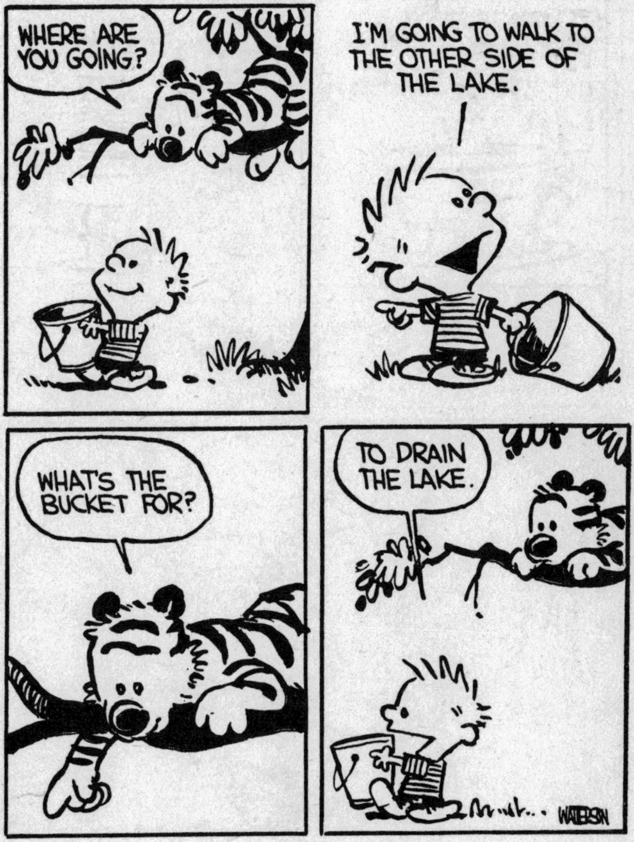
WHERE ARE YOU GOING?
I'M GOING TO WALK TO THE OTHER SIDE OF THE LAKE.
WHAT'S THE BUCKET FOR?
TO DRAIN THE LAKE.
WATTERSON

YOU KNOW WHAT I LIKE ABOUT SUMMER DAYS?
THEY'RE JUST MADE FOR *DOING* THINGS.
...EVEN IF IT'S NOTHING.
*ESPECIALLY* IF IT'S NOTHING.
WATTERSON

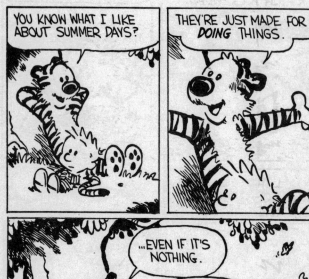

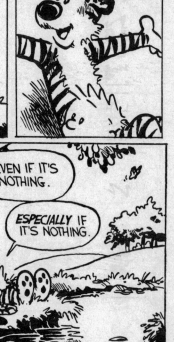

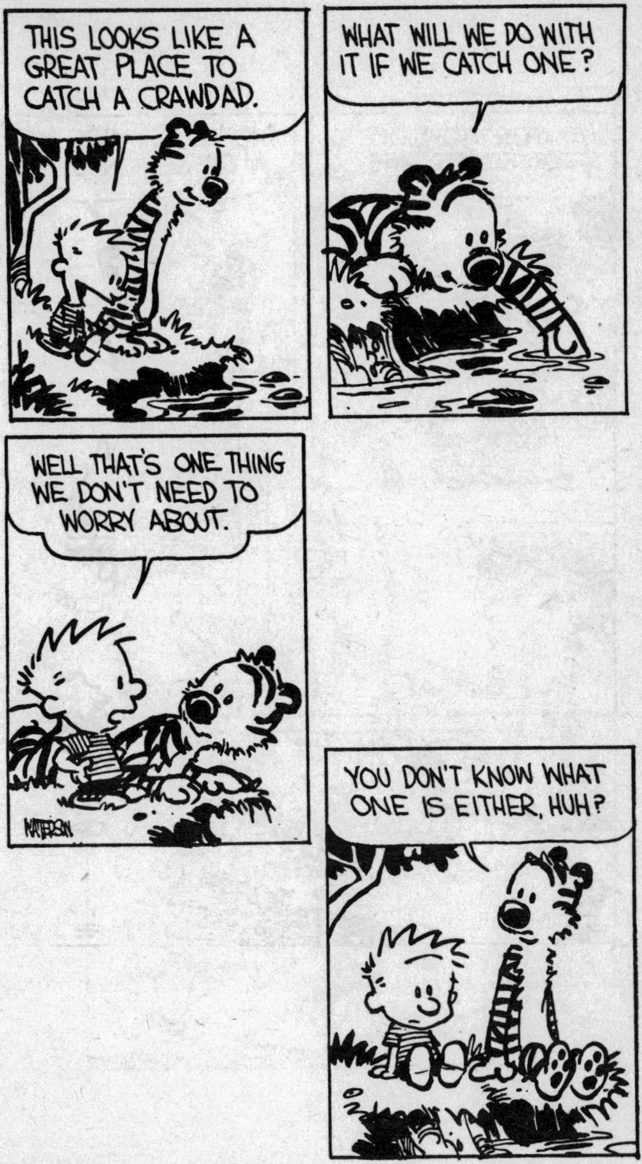
THIS LOOKS LIKE A GREAT PLACE TO CATCH A CRAWDAD.
WHAT WILL WE DO WITH IT IF WE CATCH ONE?
WELL THAT'S ONE THING WE DON'T NEED TO WORRY ABOUT.
YOU DON'T KNOW WHAT ONE IS EITHER, HUH?

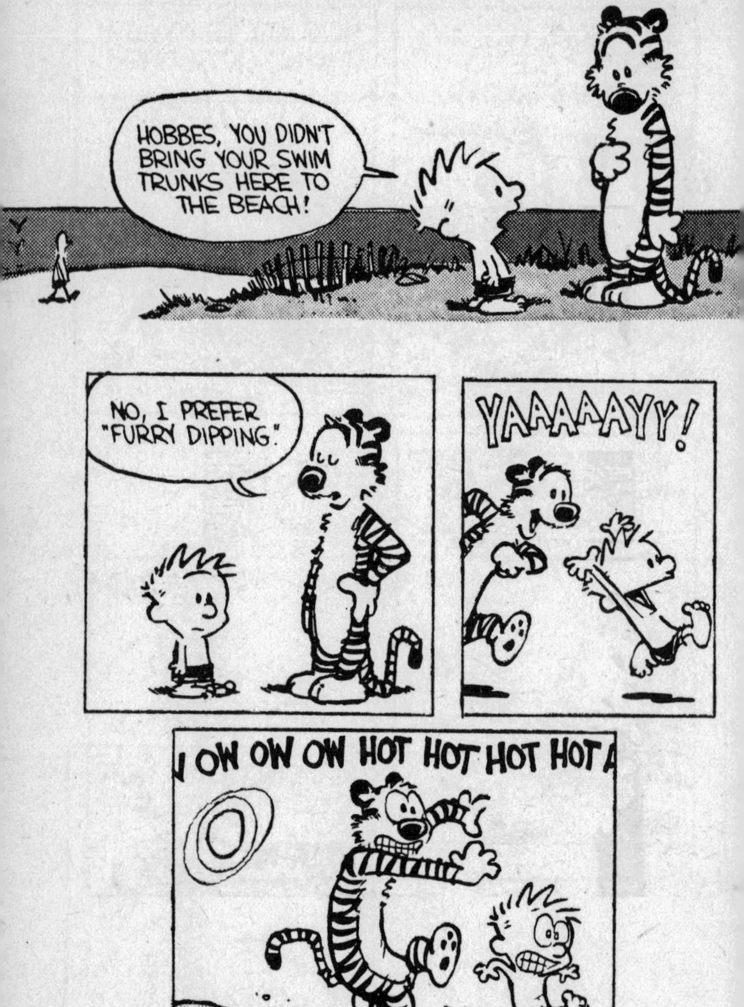
HOBBES, YOU DIDN'T BRING YOUR SWIM TRUNKS HERE TO THE BEACH!
NO, I PREFER "FURRY DIPPING."
YAAAAAYY!
OW OW OW HOT HOT HOT HOT

AAAAAAHHHHHHH
SPLOOP
SPLOP
BBBRRRR! COLD COLD COLD

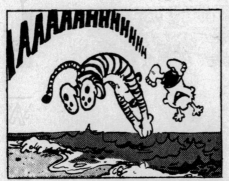

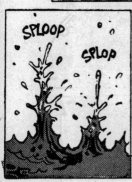

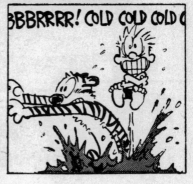

OW OW OW HOT HOT HOT HOT HOT
DON'T TELL ME WE DROVE AN HOUR AND A HALF FOR *THIS*!
WATTERSON

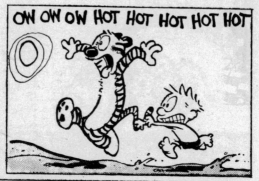

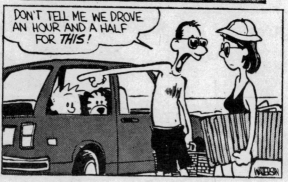

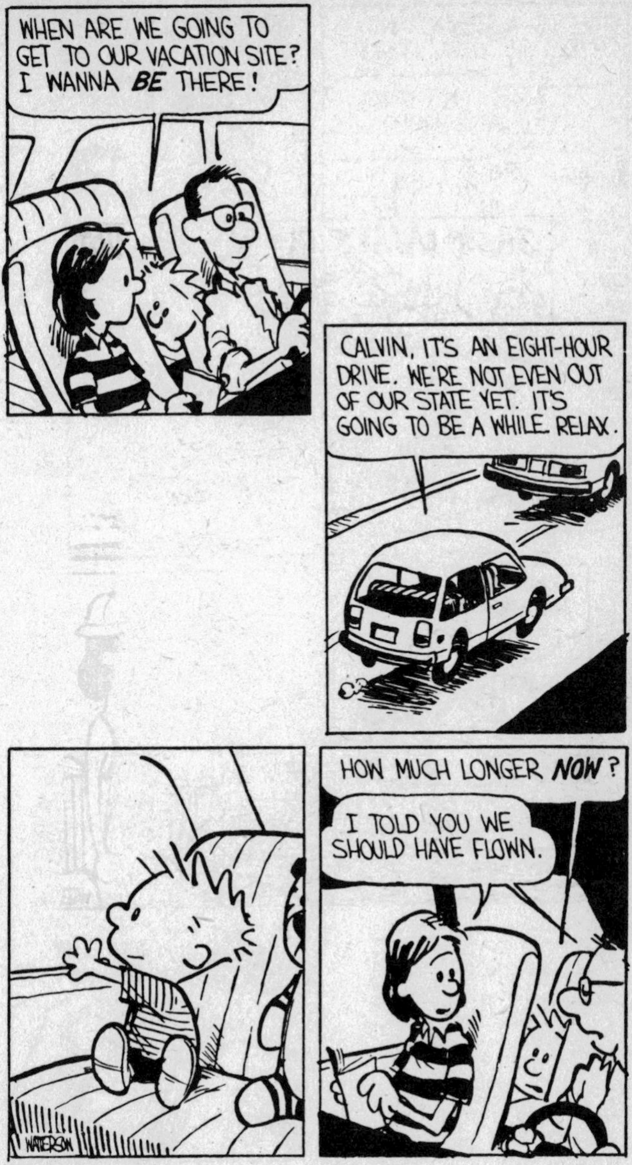
WHEN ARE WE GOING TO GET TO OUR VACATION SITE? I WANNA BE THERE!
CALVIN, IT'S AN EIGHT-HOUR DRIVE. WE'RE NOT EVEN OUT OF OUR STATE YET. IT'S GOING TO BE A WHILE. RELAX.
WATERSON
HOW MUCH LONGER NOW?
I TOLD YOU WE SHOULD HAVE FLOWN.

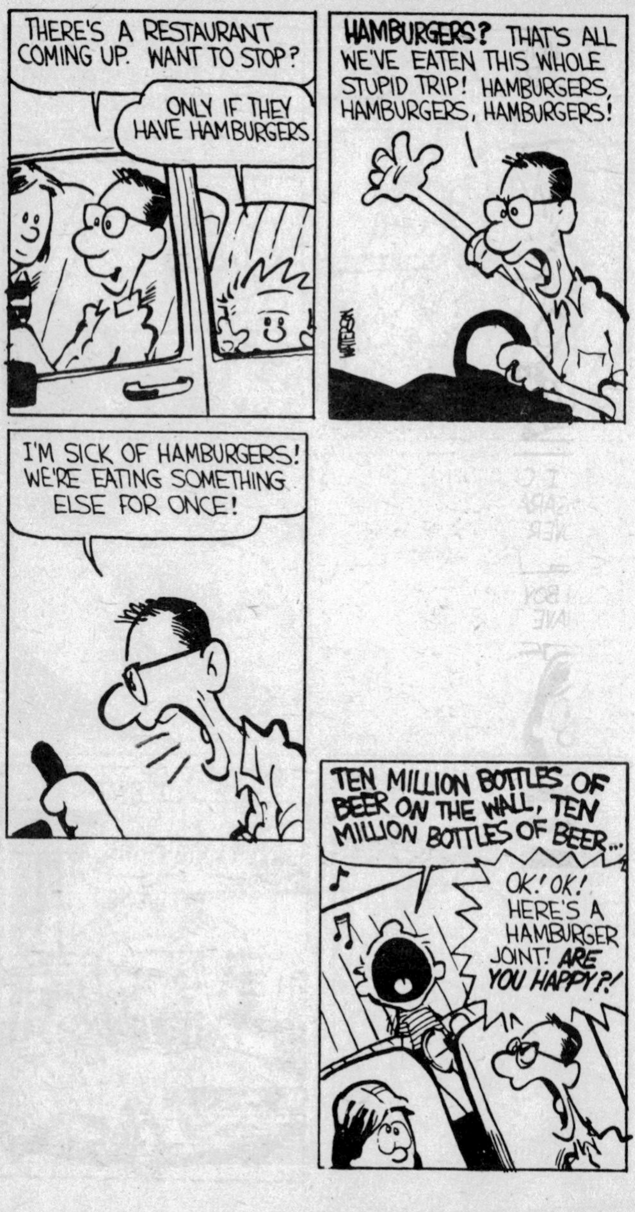
THERE'S A RESTAURANT COMING UP. WANT TO STOP?
ONLY IF THEY HAVE HAMBURGERS.
HAMBURGERS? THAT'S ALL WE'VE EATEN THIS WHOLE STUPID TRIP! HAMBURGERS, HAMBURGERS, HAMBURGERS!
I'M SICK OF HAMBURGERS! WE'RE EATING SOMETHING ELSE FOR ONCE!
TEN MILLION BOTTLES OF BEER ON THE WALL, TEN MILLION BOTTLES OF BEER...
OK! OK! HERE'S A HAMBURGER JOINT! ARE YOU HAPPY?!

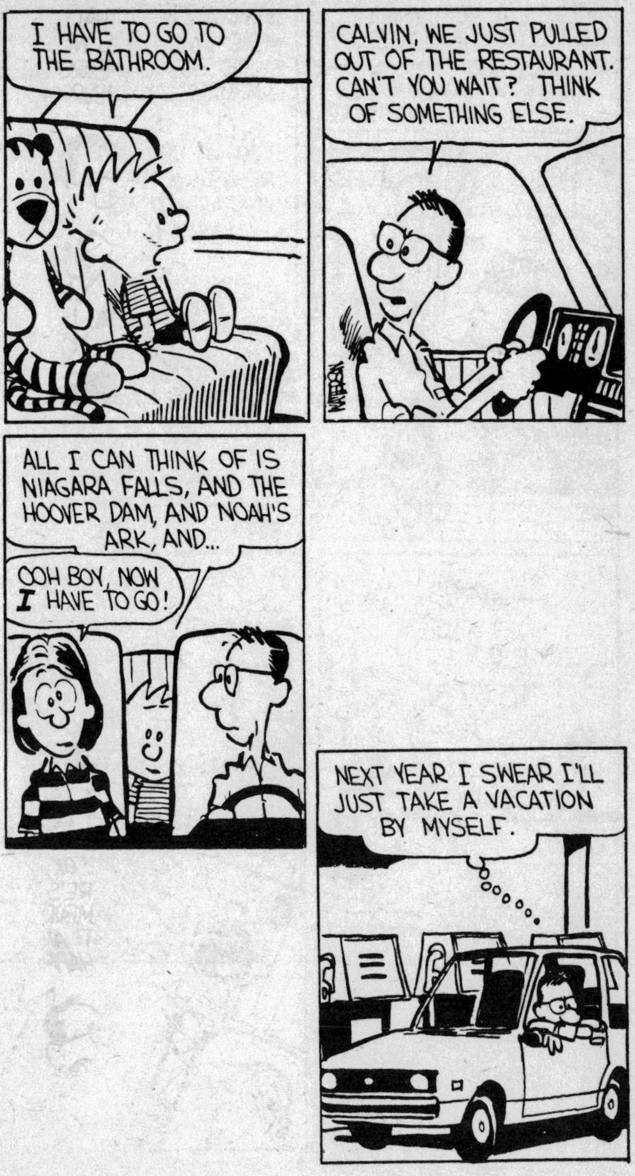
I HAVE TO GO TO THE BATHROOM.
CALVIN, WE JUST PULLED OUT OF THE RESTAURANT. CAN'T YOU WAIT? THINK OF SOMETHING ELSE.
ALL I CAN THINK OF IS NIAGARA FALLS, AND THE HOOVER DAM, AND NOAH'S ARK, AND...
OOH BOY, NOW I HAVE TO GO!
NEXT YEAR I SWEAR I'LL JUST TAKE A VACATION BY MYSELF.

THAT TRIP WAS EXCRUCIATING. THANK GOODNESS WE'RE HERE.
EIGHT HOURS CRAMMED IN A CAR WITH A HYPERACTIVE SIX-YEAR-OLD! WHAT AN ORDEAL!
WATERSON
WELL, NOW CALVIN CAN RUN AND SCREAM ALL HE LIKES. AHH, WHAT A GREAT LITTLE PLACE.
I'M BORED. WHEN ARE WE LEAVING?
YOU'RE BORED? WOULD YOU LIKE ME TO SHOW YOU HOW AN ANCHOR WORKS?

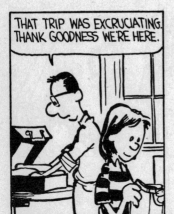

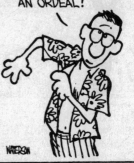

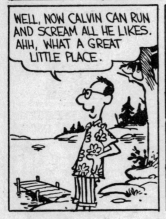

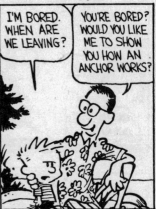

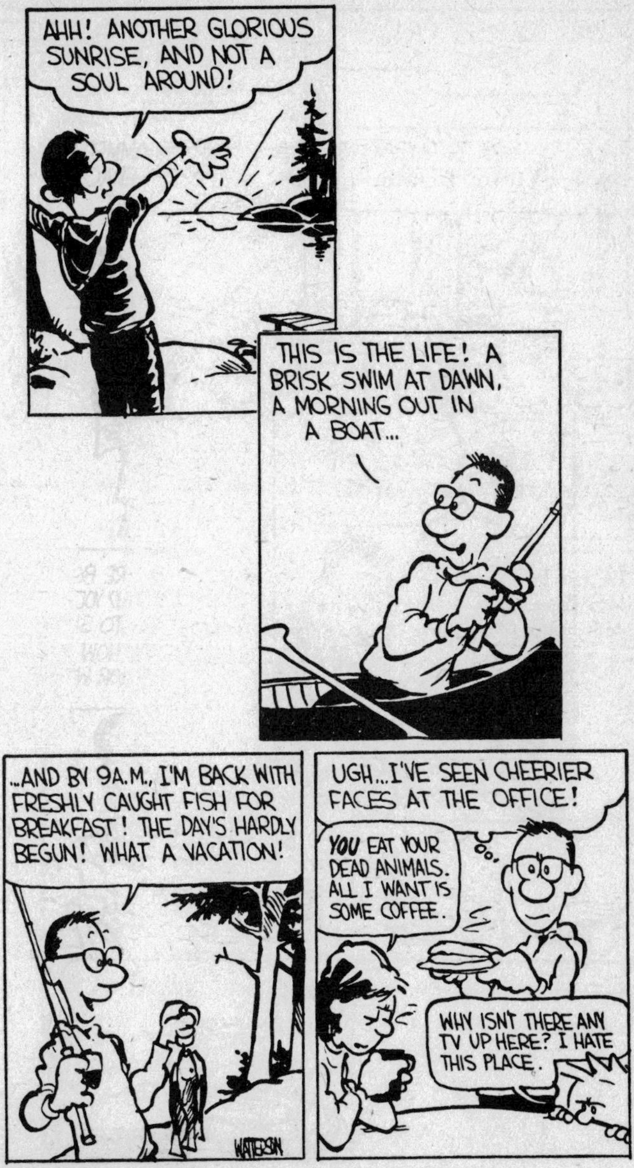
AHH! ANOTHER GLORIOUS SUNRISE, AND NOT A SOUL AROUND!
THIS IS THE LIFE! A BRISK SWIM AT DAWN, A MORNING OUT IN A BOAT...
...AND BY 9A.M., I'M BACK WITH FRESHLY CAUGHT FISH FOR BREAKFAST! THE DAY'S HARDLY BEGUN! WHAT A VACATION!
WATTERSON
UGH...I'VE SEEN CHEERIER FACES AT THE OFFICE!
YOU EAT YOUR DEAD ANIMALS. ALL I WANT IS SOME COFFEE.
WHY ISN'T THERE ANY TV UP HERE? I HATE THIS PLACE.

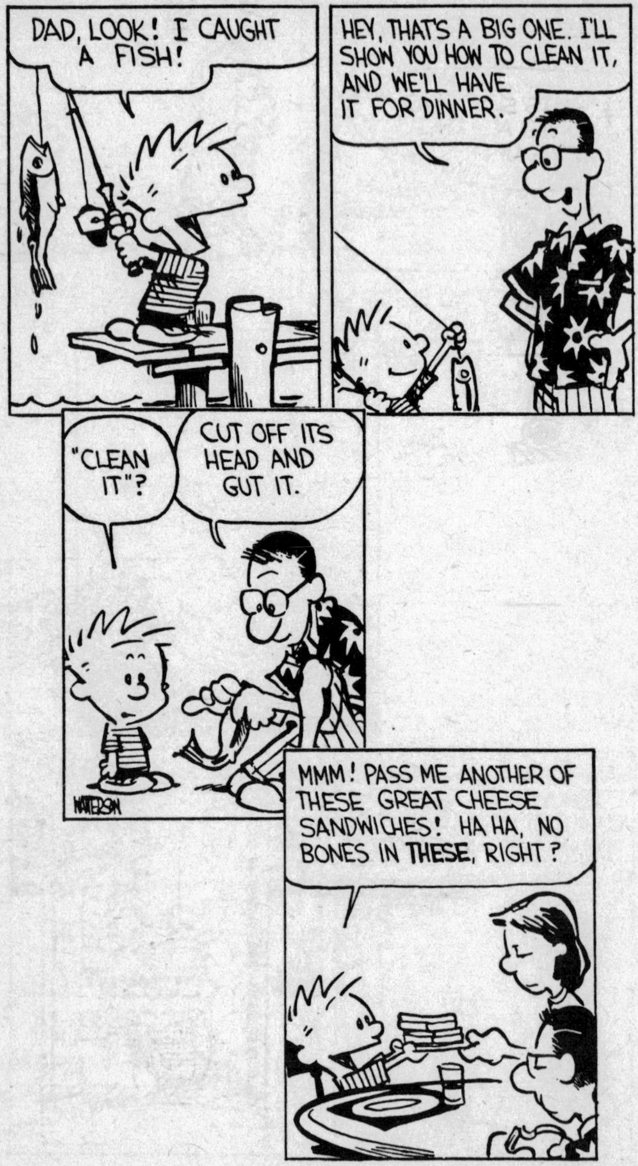
DAD, LOOK! I CAUGHT A FISH!
HEY, THAT'S A BIG ONE. I'LL SHOW YOU HOW TO CLEAN IT, AND WE'LL HAVE IT FOR DINNER.
"CLEAN IT"?
CUT OFF ITS HEAD AND GUT IT.
WATTERSON
MMM! PASS ME ANOTHER OF THESE GREAT CHEESE SANDWICHES! HA HA, NO BONES IN THESE, RIGHT?

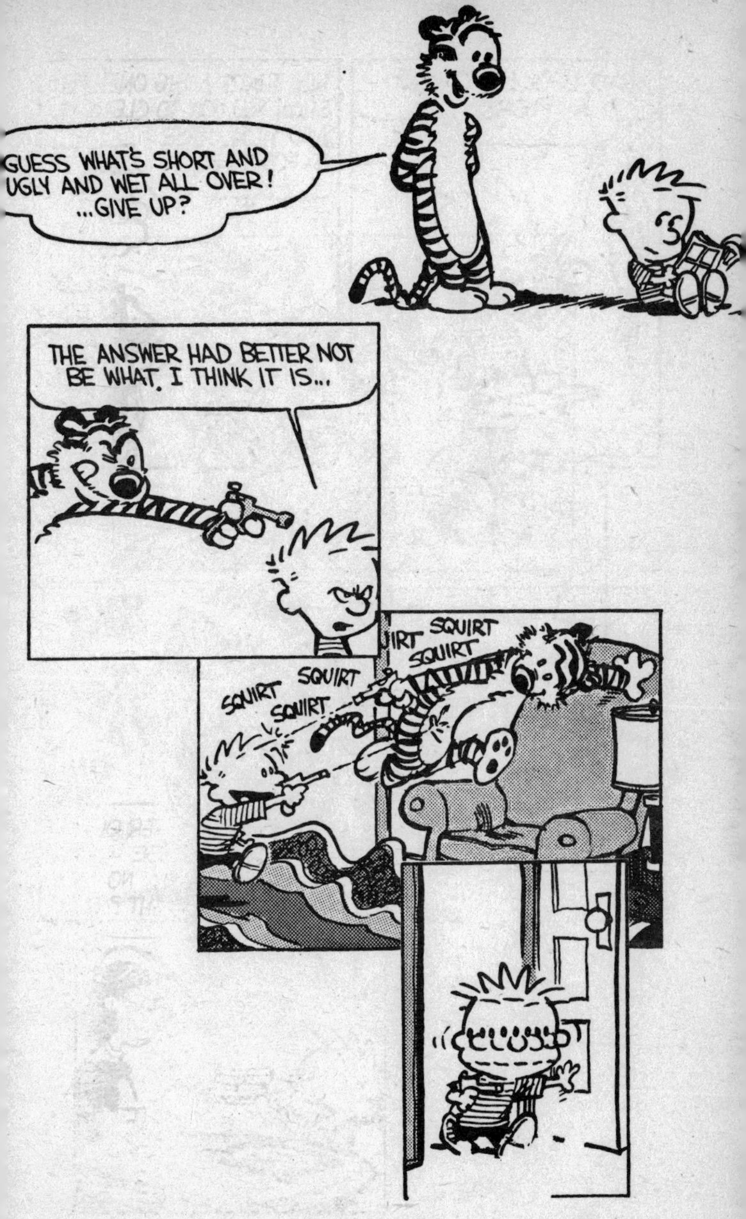
GUESS WHAT'S SHORT AND UGLY AND WET ALL OVER! ...GIVE UP?
THE ANSWER HAD BETTER NOT BE WHAT I THINK IT IS...
SQUIRT
SQUIRT
SQUIRT
SQUIRT
SQUIRT
IRT SQUIRT

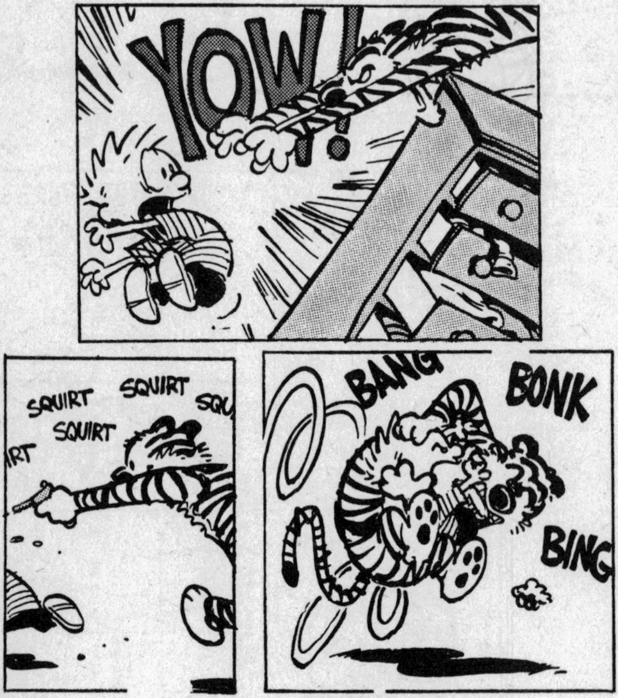
YOW!!
SQUIRT
SQUIRT
SQUIRT
BANG
BONK
BING

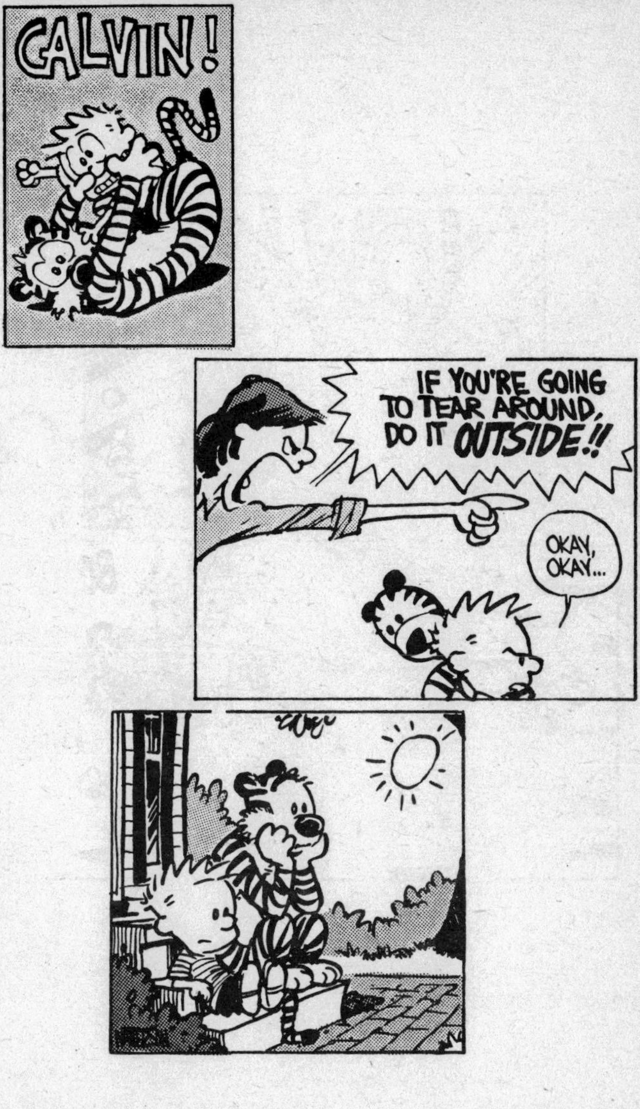
CALVIN!
IF YOU'RE GOING TO TEAR AROUND, DO IT OUTSIDE!!
OKAY, OKAY...

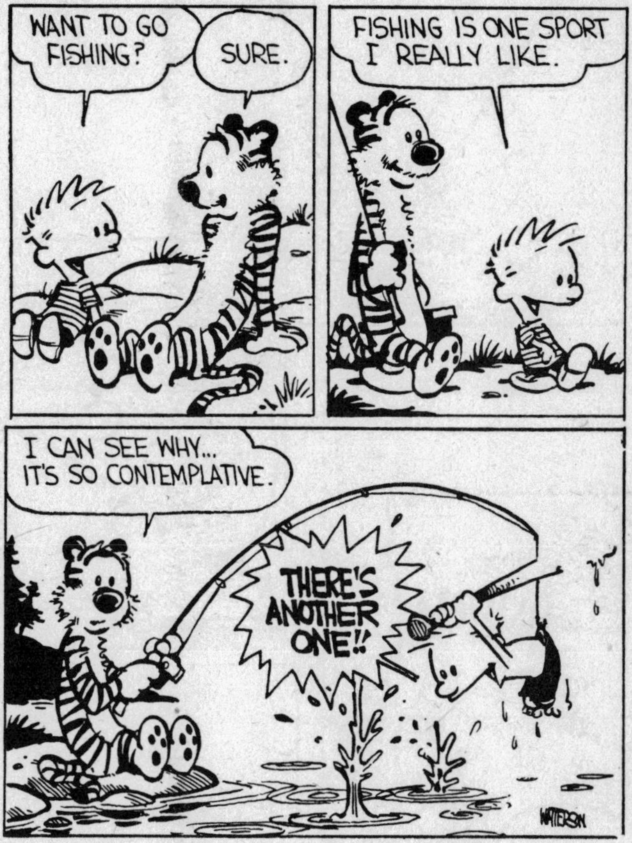
WANT TO GO FISHING?
SURE.
FISHING IS ONE SPORT I REALLY LIKE.
I CAN SEE WHY... IT'S SO CONTEMPLATIVE.
THERE'S ANOTHER ONE!!
WATTERSON

GZZZZZZZZZZZZZZ

WAAAUUGHHH!
SPLOOSH

WATTERSON

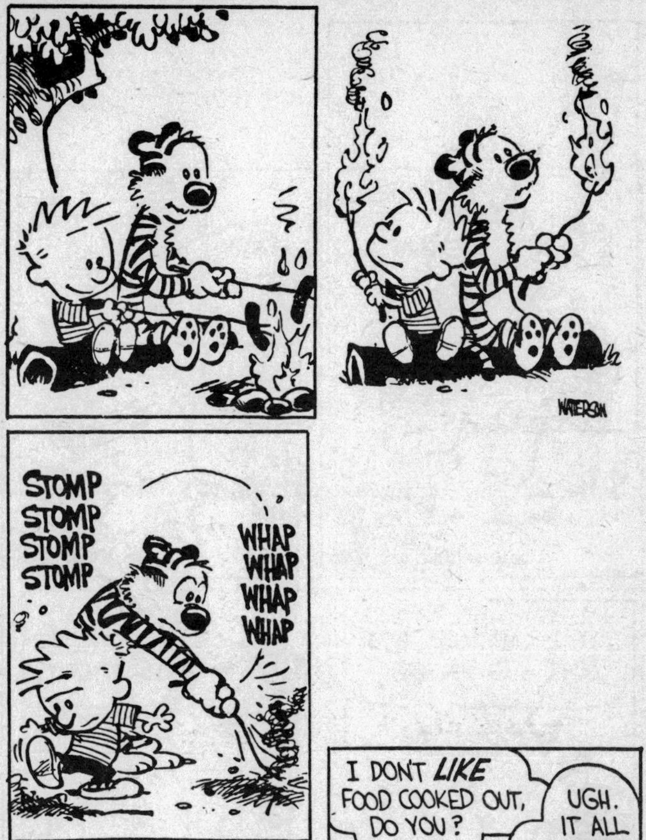
STOMP
STOMP
STOMP
STOMP
WHAP
WHAP
WHAP
WHAP
I DON'T *LIKE* FOOD COOKED OUT, DO YOU?
UGH. IT ALL TASTES THE SAME.
CRUNCH
CRUNCH

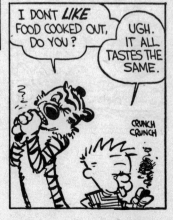

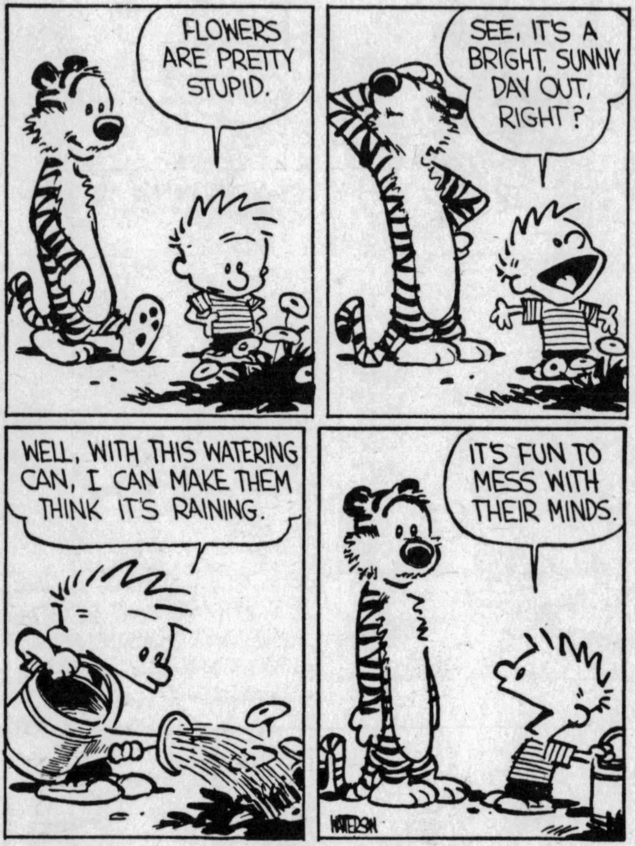
FLOWERS ARE PRETTY STUPID.
SEE, IT'S A BRIGHT, SUNNY DAY OUT, RIGHT?
WELL, WITH THIS WATERING CAN, I CAN MAKE THEM THINK IT'S RAINING.
IT'S FUN TO MESS WITH THEIR MINDS.
WATERSON

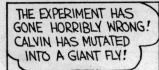

THE EXPERIMENT HAS GONE HORRIBLY WRONG! CALVIN HAS MUTATED INTO A GIANT FLY!

HE ZIPS ABOUT IN PARASITIC HUNGER, SEARCHING FOR DECAYING FLESH!

AN UNBEARABLE STENCH FILLS THE AIR. THE HIDEOUS BUG ZEROES IN.

MMM! THIS MAKES ME HUNGRY!

DON'T BE GROSS. JUST TAKE OUT THE GARBAGE LIKE I ASKED YOU, WILL YOU PLEASE?

WATTERSON

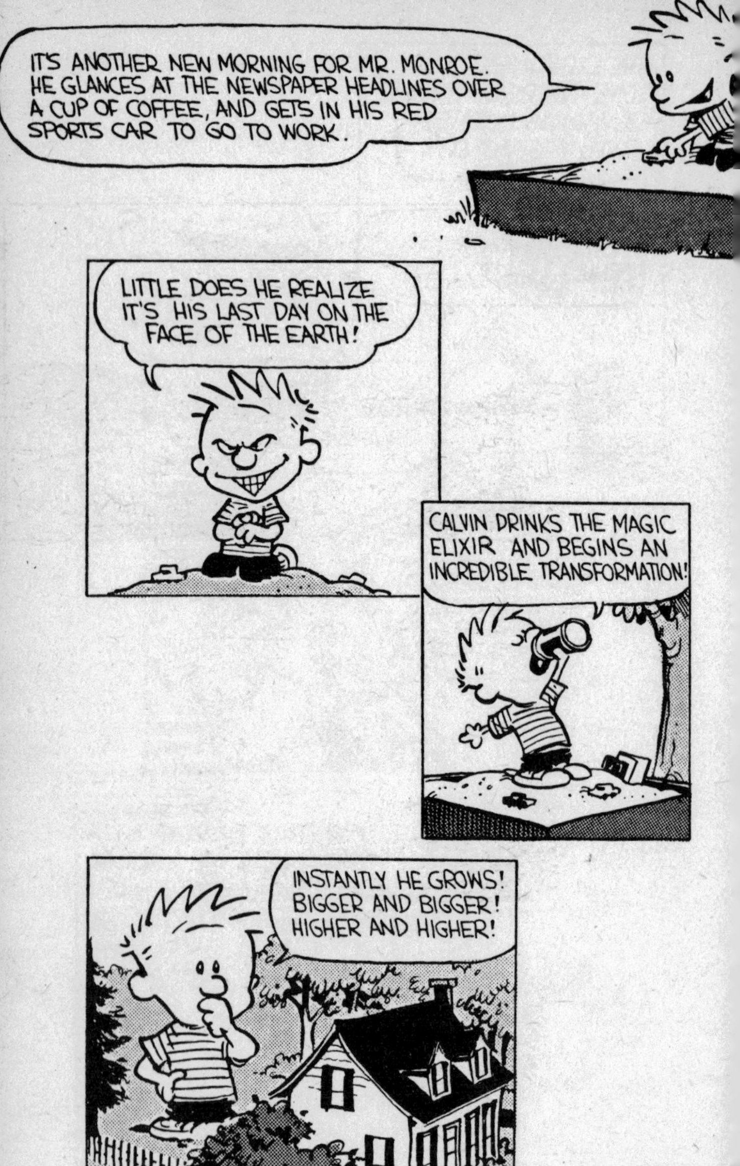
IT'S ANOTHER NEW MORNING FOR MR. MONROE. HE GLANCES AT THE NEWSPAPER HEADLINES OVER A CUP OF COFFEE, AND GETS IN HIS RED SPORTS CAR TO GO TO WORK.
LITTLE DOES HE REALIZE IT'S HIS LAST DAY ON THE FACE OF THE EARTH!
CALVIN DRINKS THE MAGIC ELIXIR AND BEGINS AN INCREDIBLE TRANSFORMATION!
INSTANTLY HE GROWS! BIGGER AND BIGGER! HIGHER AND HIGHER!

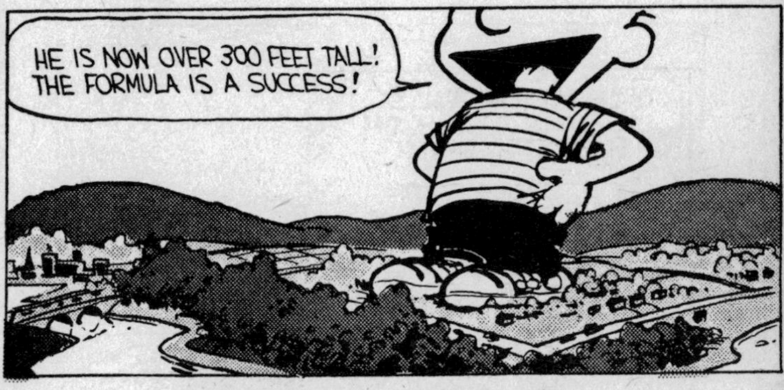
HE IS NOW OVER 300 FEET TALL! THE FORMULA IS A SUCCESS!

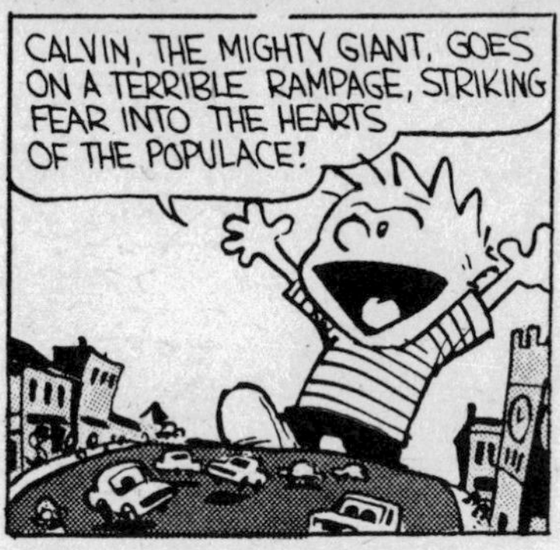
CALVIN, THE MIGHTY GIANT, GOES ON A TERRIBLE RAMPAGE, STRIKING FEAR INTO THE HEARTS OF THE POPULACE!

NOTHING CAN STOP HIM! IT'S PANIC IN THE STREETS! A TOWN LIES IN RUINS!
NO, I WON'T BUY YOU ANY MORE TOY CARS. I SAW YOU! YOU DELIBERATELY STOMPED ON THOSE!
WATTERSON

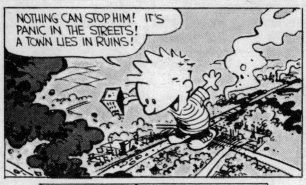

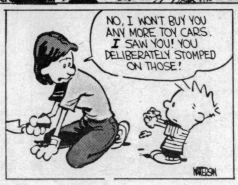

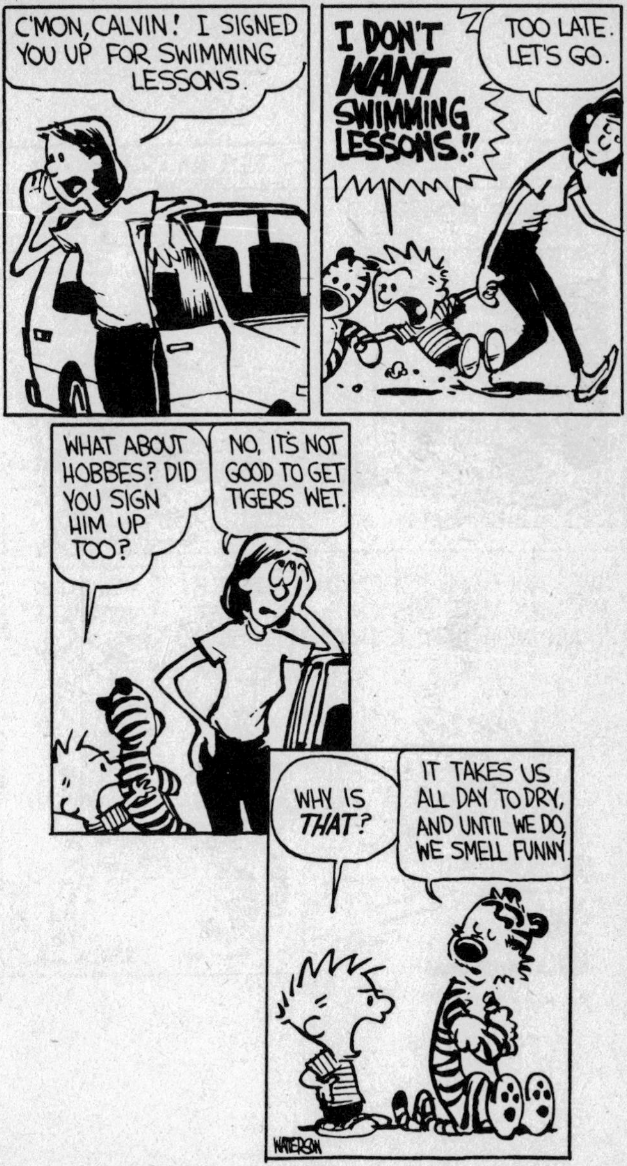
C'MON, CALVIN! I SIGNED YOU UP FOR SWIMMING LESSONS.
I DON'T *WANT* SWIMMING LESSONS!!
TOO LATE. LET'S GO.
WHAT ABOUT HOBBES? DID YOU SIGN HIM UP TOO?
NO, IT'S NOT GOOD TO GET TIGERS WET.
WHY IS *THAT*?
IT TAKES US ALL DAY TO DRY, AND UNTIL WE DO, WE SMELL FUNNY.
WATERSON

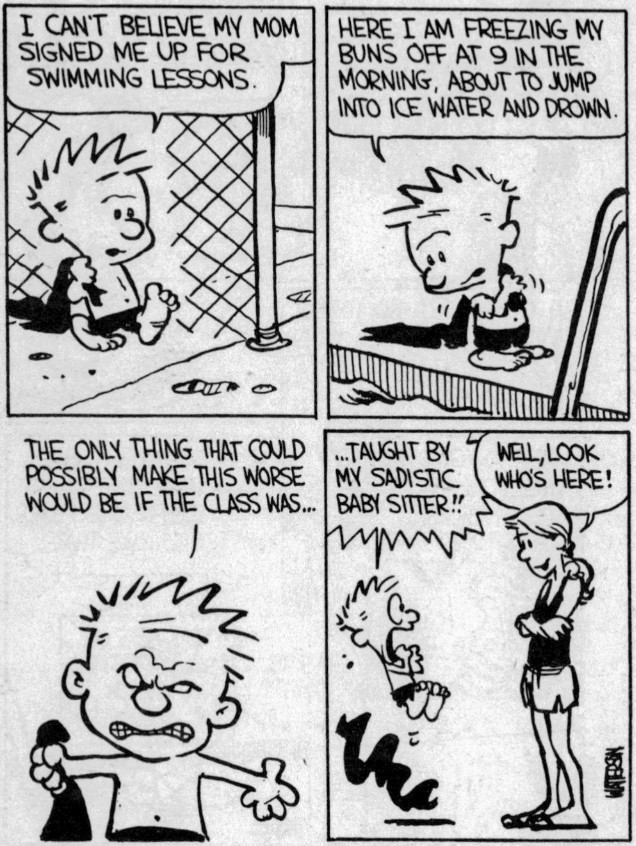
I CAN'T BELIEVE MY MOM SIGNED ME UP FOR SWIMMING LESSONS.
HERE I AM FREEZING MY BUNS OFF AT 9 IN THE MORNING, ABOUT TO JUMP INTO ICE WATER AND DROWN.
THE ONLY THING THAT COULD POSSIBLY MAKE THIS WORSE WOULD BE IF THE CLASS WAS...
...TAUGHT BY MY SADISTIC BABY SITTER!!
WELL, LOOK WHO'S HERE!
WATERSON

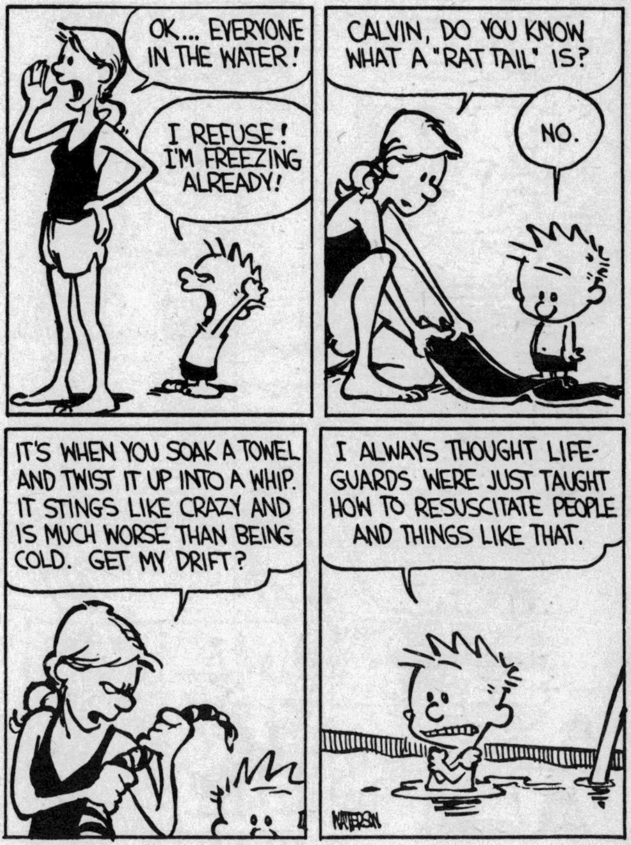
OK... EVERYONE IN THE WATER!
I REFUSE! I'M FREEZING ALREADY!
CALVIN, DO YOU KNOW WHAT A "RAT TAIL" IS?
NO.
IT'S WHEN YOU SOAK A TOWEL AND TWIST IT UP INTO A WHIP. IT STINGS LIKE CRAZY AND IS MUCH WORSE THAN BEING COLD. GET MY DRIFT?
I ALWAYS THOUGHT LIFE-GUARDS WERE JUST TAUGHT HOW TO RESUSCITATE PEOPLE AND THINGS LIKE THAT.
WATTERSON

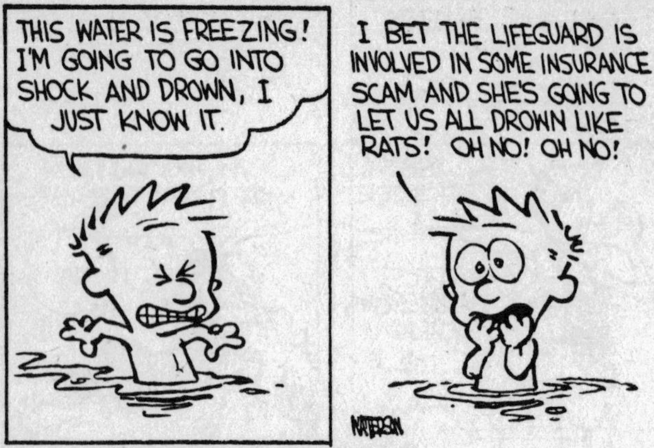
THIS WATER IS FREEZING! I'M GOING TO GO INTO SHOCK AND DROWN, I JUST KNOW IT.
I BET THE LIFEGUARD IS INVOLVED IN SOME INSURANCE SCAM AND SHE'S GOING TO LET US ALL DROWN LIKE RATS! OH NO! OH NO!

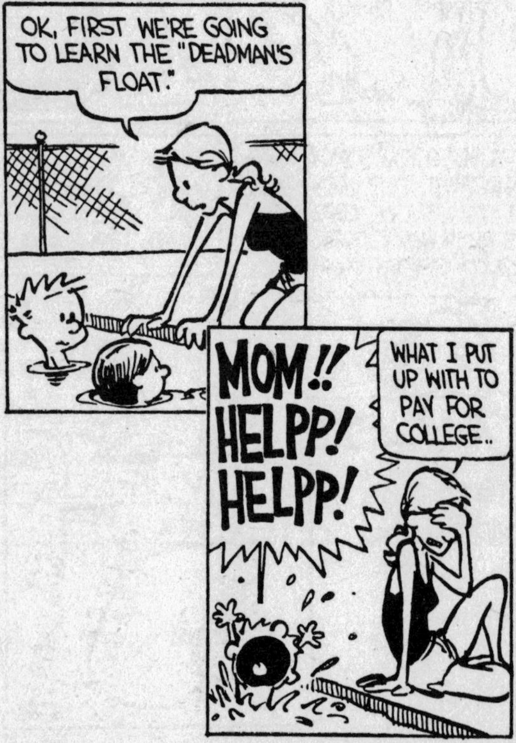
OK, FIRST WE'RE GOING TO LEARN THE "DEADMAN'S FLOAT."
MOM!! HELPP! HELPP!
WHAT I PUT UP WITH TO PAY FOR COLLEGE..

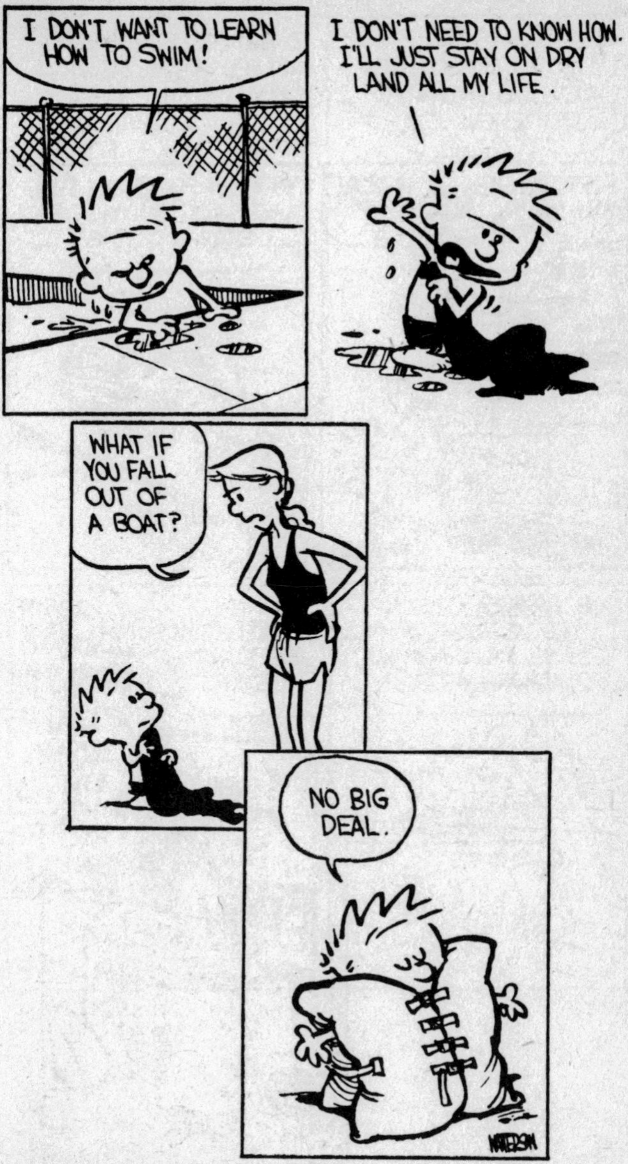
I DON'T WANT TO LEARN HOW TO SWIM!
I DON'T NEED TO KNOW HOW. I'LL JUST STAY ON DRY LAND ALL MY LIFE.
WHAT IF YOU FALL OUT OF A BOAT?
NO BIG DEAL.
WATERSON

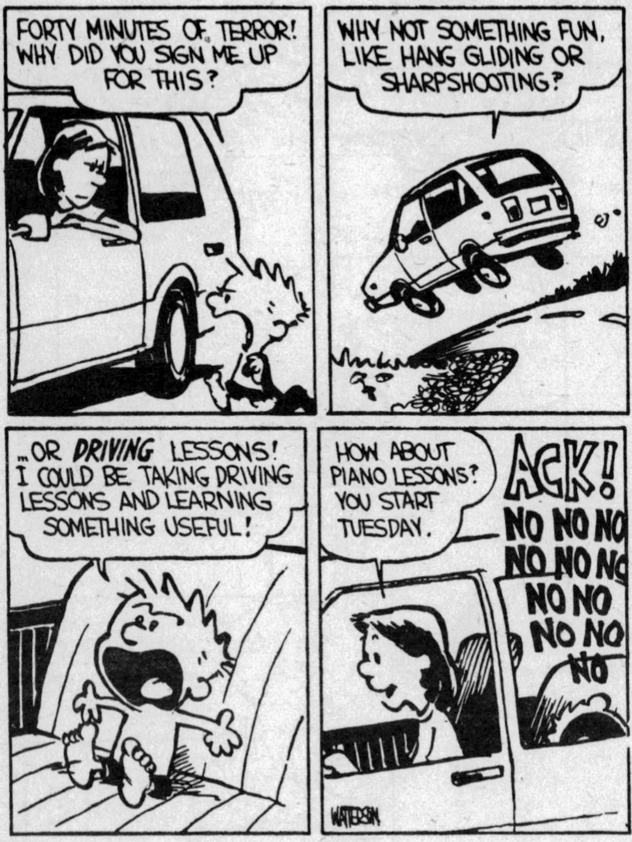
FORTY MINUTES OF TERROR! WHY DID YOU SIGN ME UP FOR THIS?
WHY NOT SOMETHING FUN, LIKE HANG GLIDING OR SHARPSHOOTING?
...OR DRIVING LESSONS! I COULD BE TAKING DRIVING LESSONS AND LEARNING SOMETHING USEFUL!
HOW ABOUT PIANO LESSONS? YOU START TUESDAY.
ACK!
NO NO NO NO NO NO NO NO NO NO NO
WATTERSON

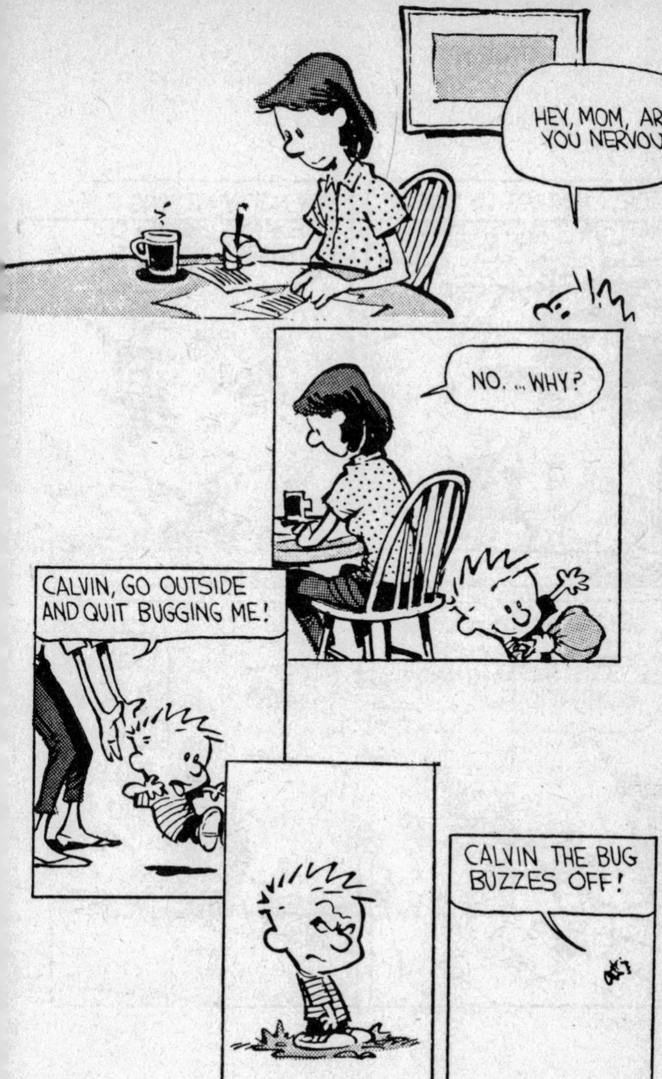
HEY, MOM, ARE YOU NERVOUS?
NO. ...WHY?
CALVIN, GO OUTSIDE AND QUIT BUGGING ME!
CALVIN THE BUG BUZZES OFF!

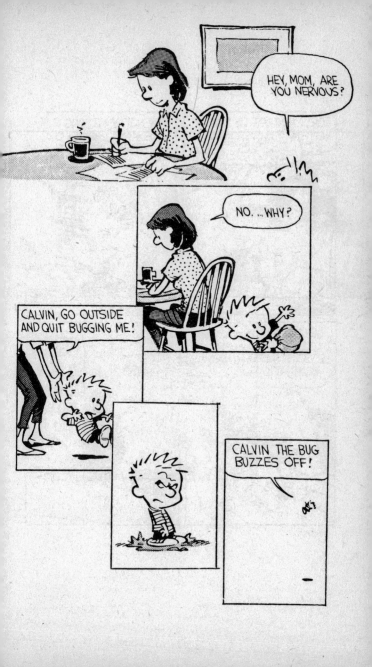

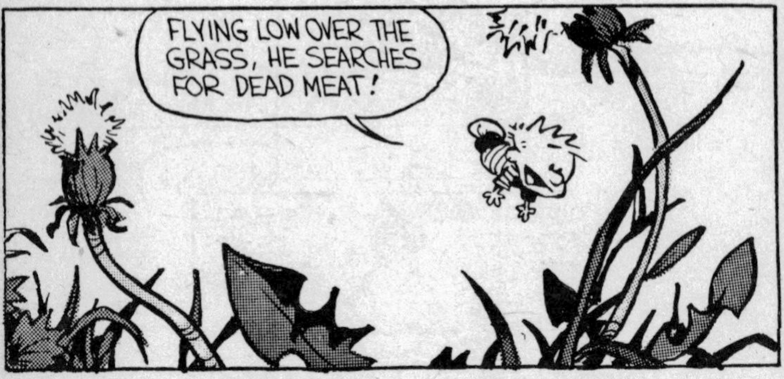
FLYING LOW OVER THE GRASS, HE SEARCHES FOR DEAD MEAT!

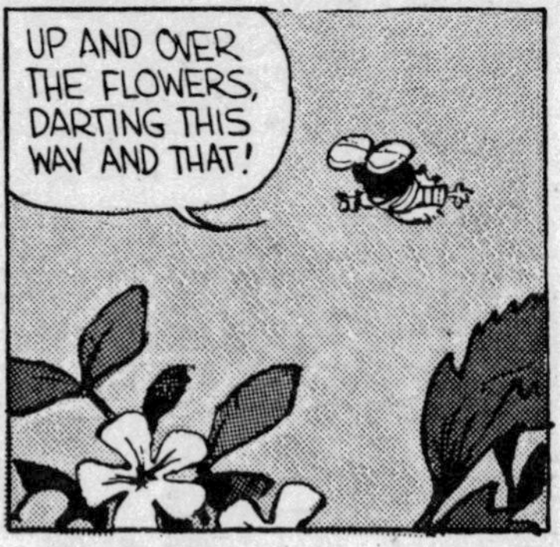
UP AND OVER THE FLOWERS, DARTING THIS WAY AND THAT!

OH NO! HE'S CAUGHT IN A SPIDER WEB!
THRASHING ABOUT IN A DESPERATE BID FOR FREEDOM, HE ONLY BECOMES MORE ENTANGLED! SOON THE SPIDER WILL SUCK OUT HIS INNARDS! HELP!
WATTERSON
I WAS GOING TO JOIN YOU IN THE HAMMOCK, BUT I THINK I'LL FORGET IT.

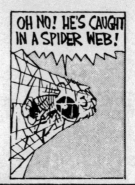

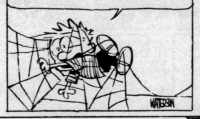

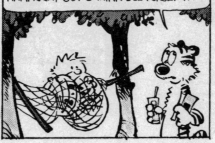

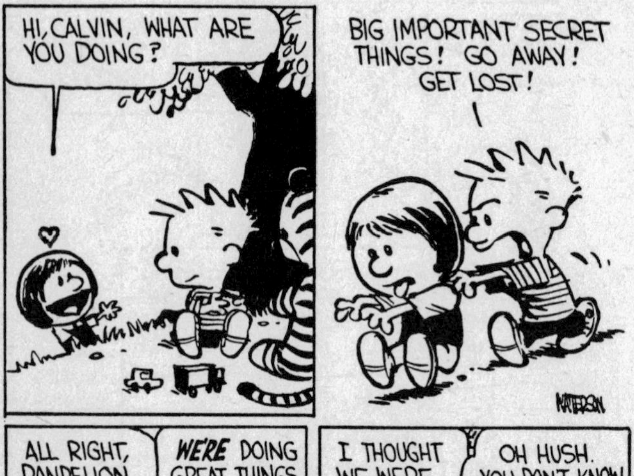

HI, CALVIN, WHAT ARE YOU DOING?
BIG IMPORTANT SECRET THINGS! GO AWAY! GET LOST!
WATTERSON
ALL RIGHT, DANDELION HEAD! WHO CARES WHAT YOU DO ANYWAY!
WE'RE DOING GREAT THINGS. WE'RE HAVING FUN!
I THOUGHT WE WERE BORED OUT OF OUR SKULLS.
OH HUSH. YOU DON'T KNOW ANYTHING.

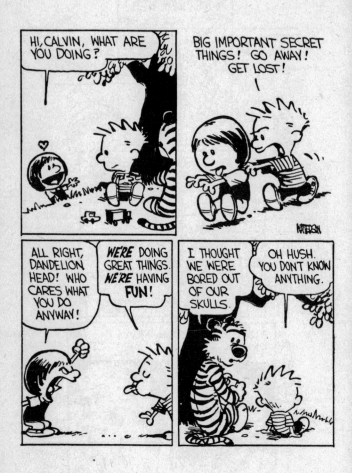

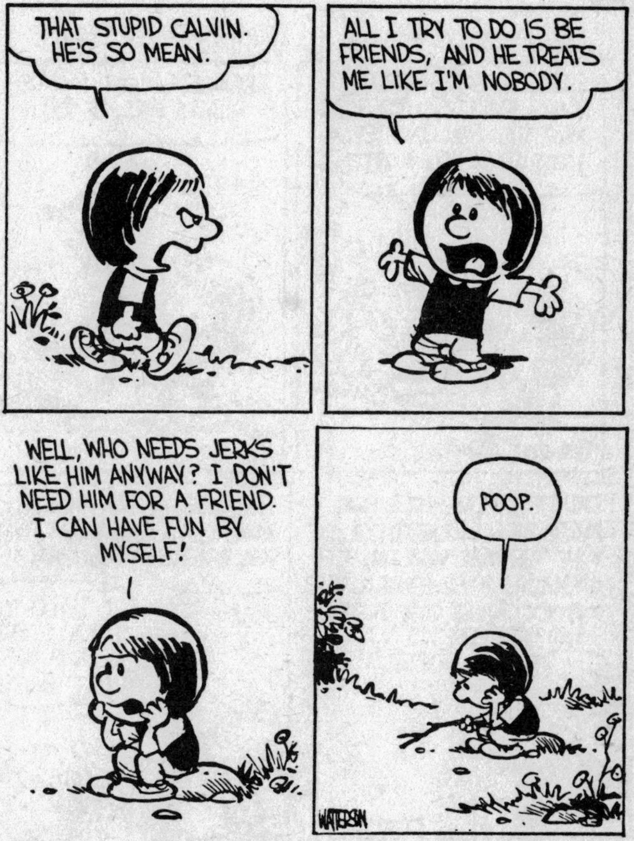
THAT STUPID CALVIN. HE'S SO MEAN.
ALL I TRY TO DO IS BE FRIENDS, AND HE TREATS ME LIKE I'M NOBODY.
WELL, WHO NEEDS JERKS LIKE HIM ANYWAY? I DON'T NEED HIM FOR A FRIEND. I CAN HAVE FUN BY MYSELF!
POOP.
WATTERSON

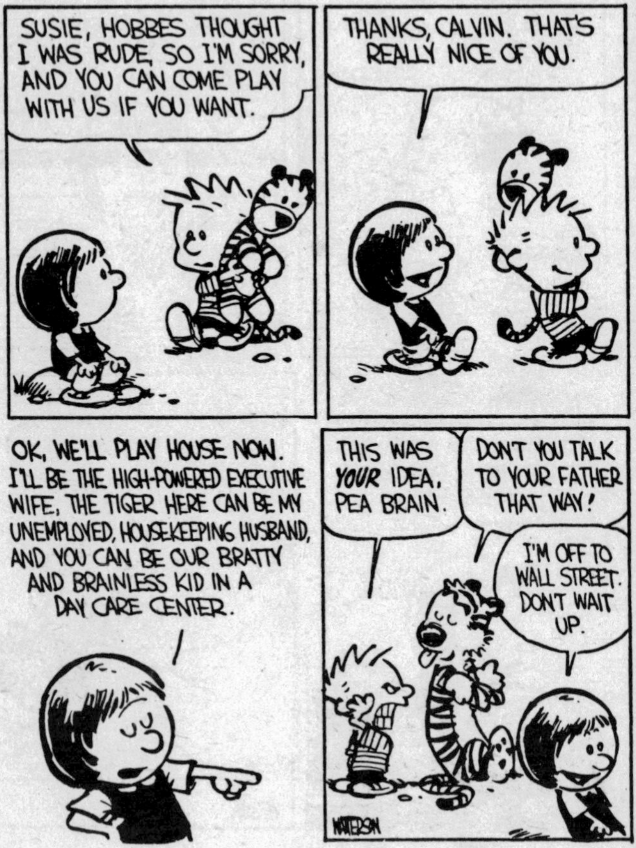
SUSIE, HOBBES THOUGHT I WAS RUDE, SO I'M SORRY, AND YOU CAN COME PLAY WITH US IF YOU WANT.
THANKS, CALVIN. THAT'S REALLY NICE OF YOU.
OK, WE'LL PLAY HOUSE NOW. I'LL BE THE HIGH-POWERED EXECUTIVE WIFE, THE TIGER HERE CAN BE MY UNEMPLOYED, HOUSEKEEPING HUSBAND, AND YOU CAN BE OUR BRATTY AND BRAINLESS KID IN A DAY CARE CENTER.
THIS WAS *YOUR* IDEA, PEA BRAIN.
DON'T YOU TALK TO YOUR FATHER THAT WAY!
I'M OFF TO WALL STREET. DON'T WAIT UP.
WATERSON

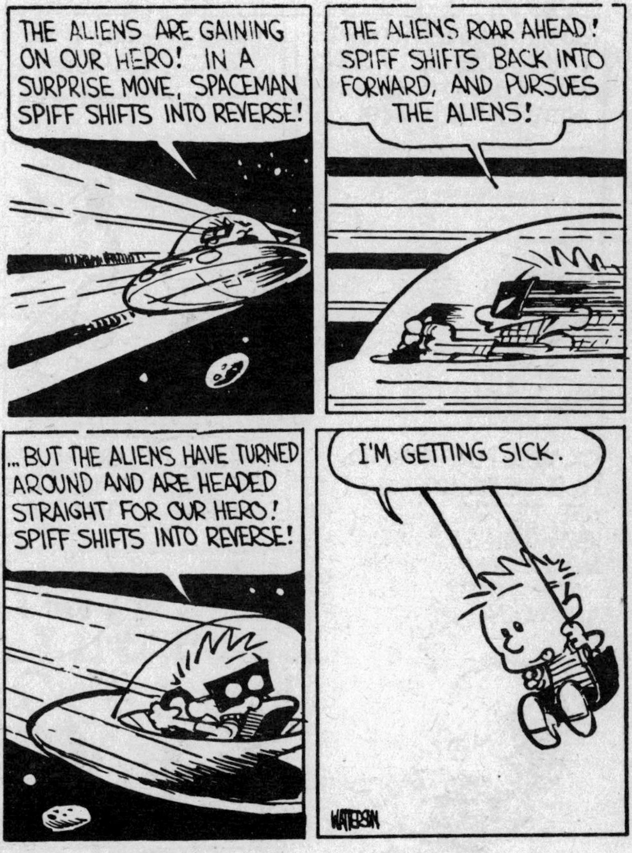
THE ALIENS ARE GAINING ON OUR HERO! IN A SURPRISE MOVE, SPACEMAN SPIFF SHIFTS INTO REVERSE!
THE ALIENS ROAR AHEAD! SPIFF SHIFTS BACK INTO FORWARD, AND PURSUES THE ALIENS!
...BUT THE ALIENS HAVE TURNED AROUND AND ARE HEADED STRAIGHT FOR OUR HERO! SPIFF SHIFTS INTO REVERSE!
I'M GETTING SICK.
WATTERSON

WHACK!

TELL ME THIS ISN'T
A SPITBALL!!

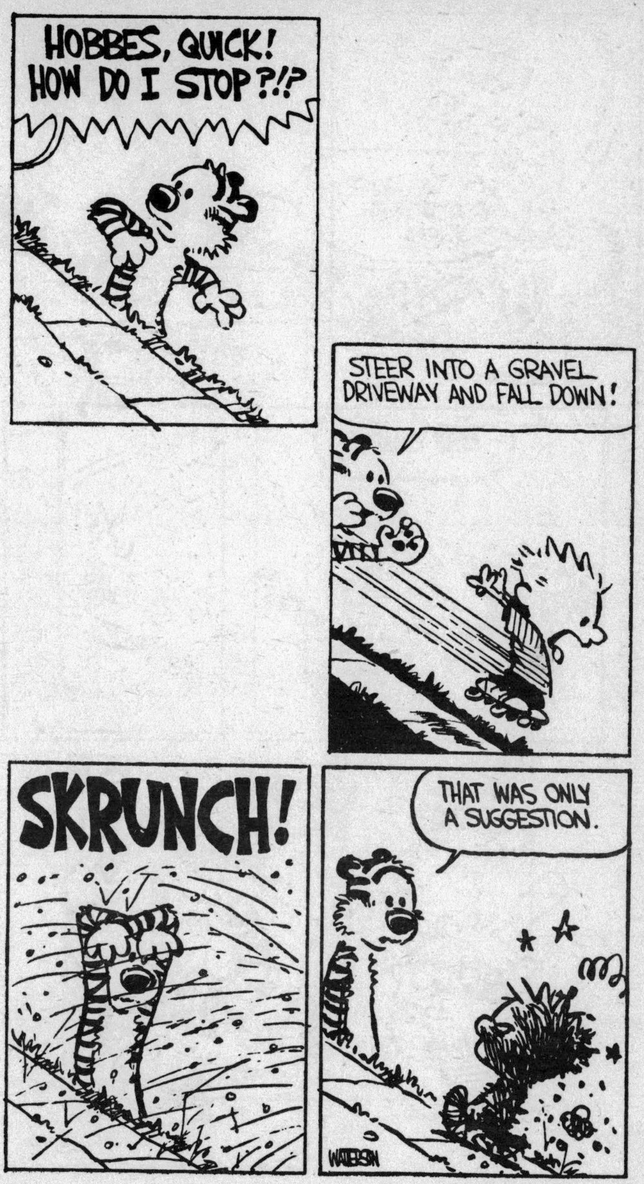
HOBBES, QUICK! HOW DO I STOP?!?
STEER INTO A GRAVEL DRIVEWAY AND FALL DOWN!
SKRUNCH!
THAT WAS ONLY A SUGGESTION.
WATTERSON

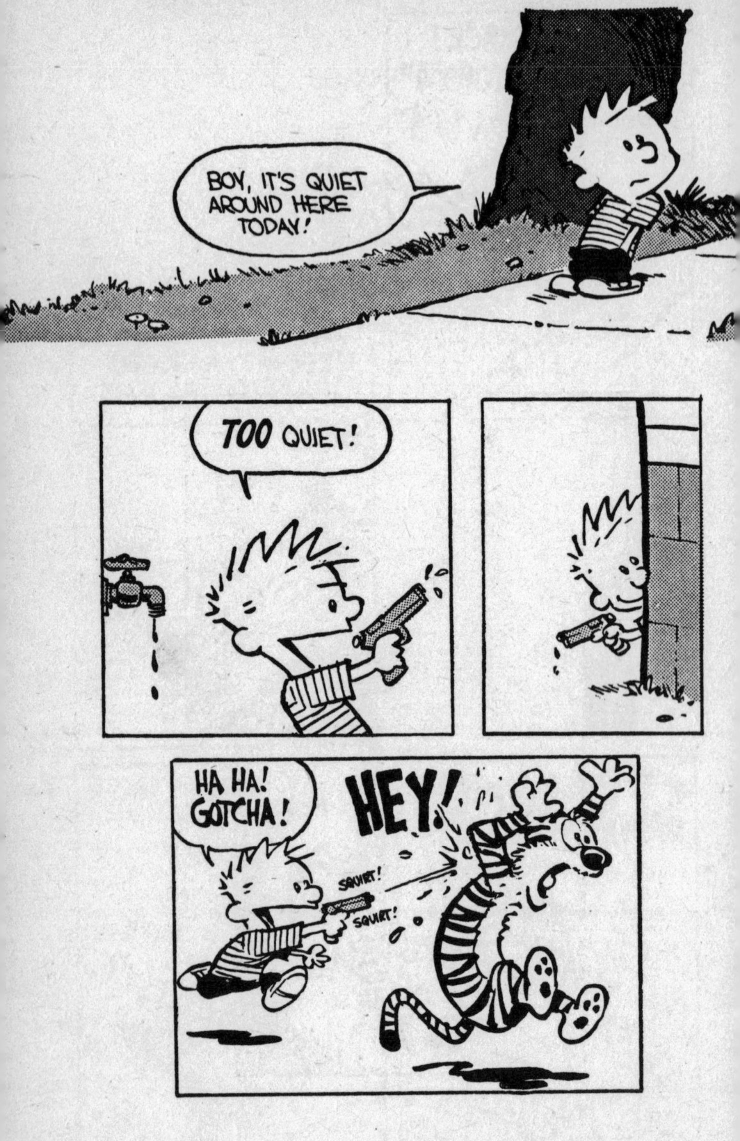
BOY, IT'S QUIET AROUND HERE TODAY!
TOO QUIET!
HA HA! GOTCHA!
HEY!
SQUIRT!
SQUIRT!

..RRRRRRRR...
SQUEAK
WHOOSH!
HA HA! GOTCHA BACK!
HEY!
SPLOOSH

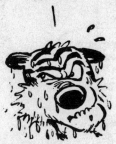

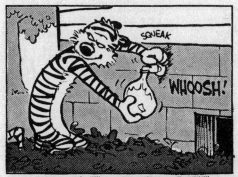

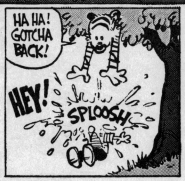

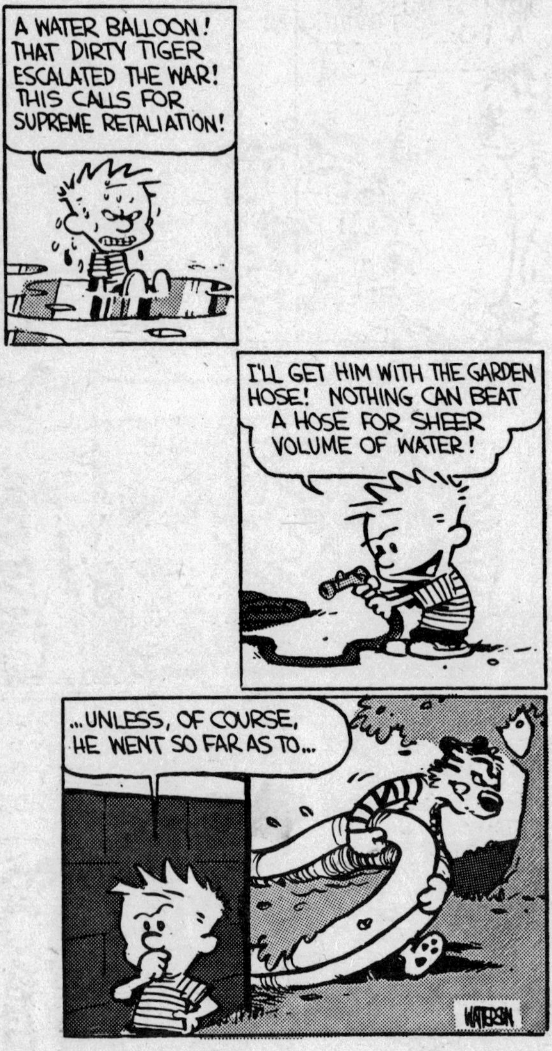
A WATER BALLOON! THAT DIRTY TIGER ESCALATED THE WAR! THIS CALLS FOR SUPREME RETALIATION!
I'LL GET HIM WITH THE GARDEN HOSE! NOTHING CAN BEAT A HOSE FOR SHEER VOLUME OF WATER!
...UNLESS, OF COURSE, HE WENT SO FAR AS TO...
WATTERSON

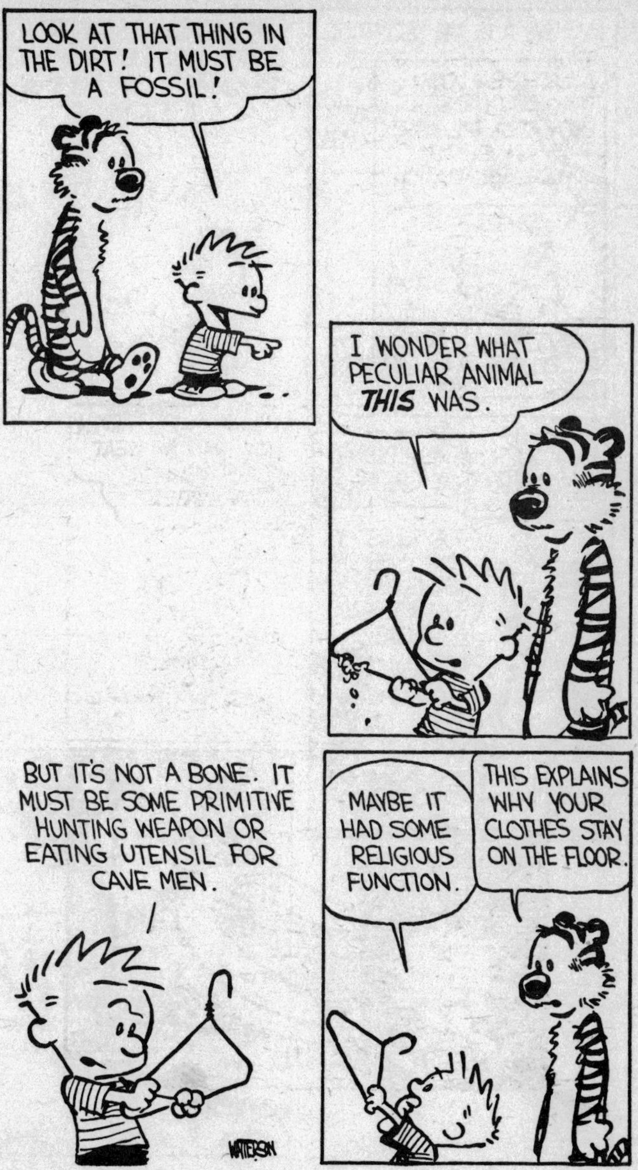
LOOK AT THAT THING IN THE DIRT! IT MUST BE A FOSSIL!
I WONDER WHAT PECULIAR ANIMAL THIS WAS.
BUT IT'S NOT A BONE. IT MUST BE SOME PRIMITIVE HUNTING WEAPON OR EATING UTENSIL FOR CAVE MEN.
WATERSON
MAYBE IT HAD SOME RELIGIOUS FUNCTION.
THIS EXPLAINS WHY YOUR CLOTHES STAY ON THE FLOOR.

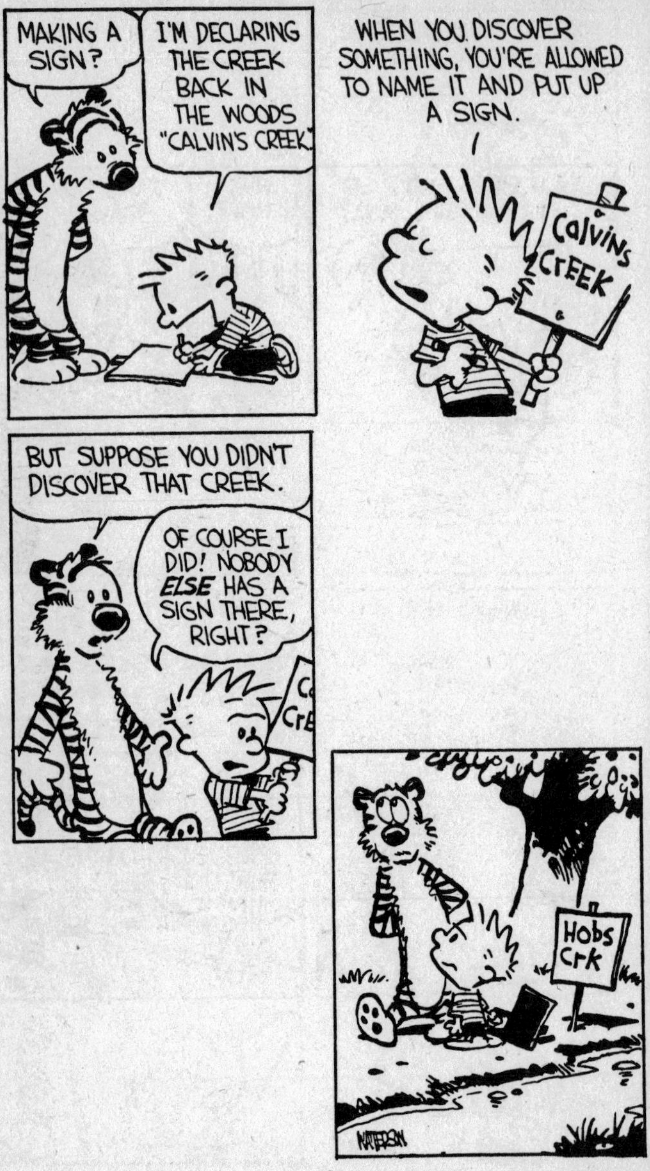
MAKING A SIGN?
I'M DECLARING THE CREEK BACK IN THE WOODS "CALVIN'S CREEK."
WHEN YOU DISCOVER SOMETHING, YOU'RE ALLOWED TO NAME IT AND PUT UP A SIGN.
Calvins CrEEK
BUT SUPPOSE YOU DIDN'T DISCOVER THAT CREEK.
OF COURSE I DID! NOBODY *ELSE* HAS A SIGN THERE, RIGHT?
Hobs Crk

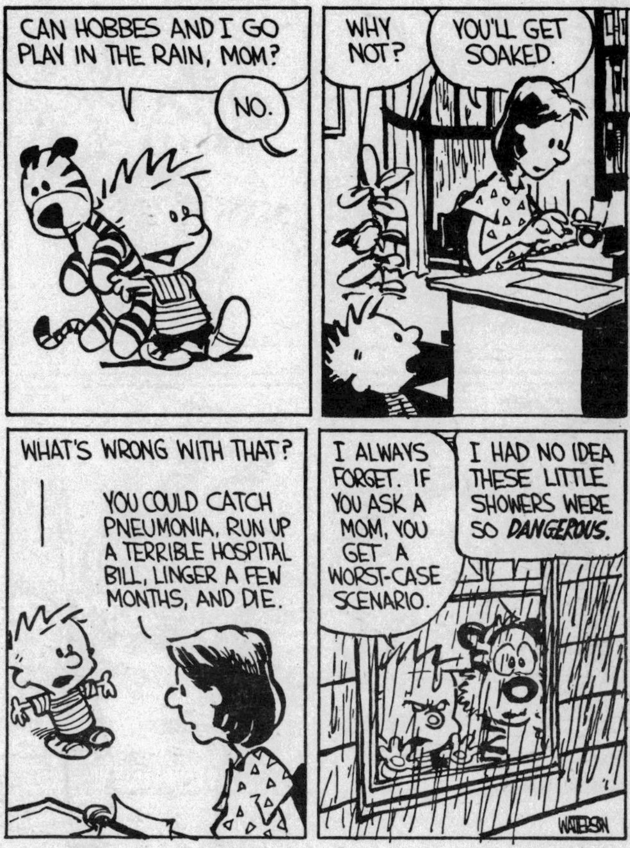
CAN HOBBES AND I GO PLAY IN THE RAIN, MOM?
NO.
WHY NOT?
YOU'LL GET SOAKED.
WHAT'S WRONG WITH THAT?
YOU COULD CATCH PNEUMONIA, RUN UP A TERRIBLE HOSPITAL BILL, LINGER A FEW MONTHS, AND DIE.
I ALWAYS FORGET. IF YOU ASK A MOM, YOU GET A WORST-CASE SCENARIO.
I HAD NO IDEA THESE LITTLE SHOWERS WERE SO DANGEROUS.
WATTERSON

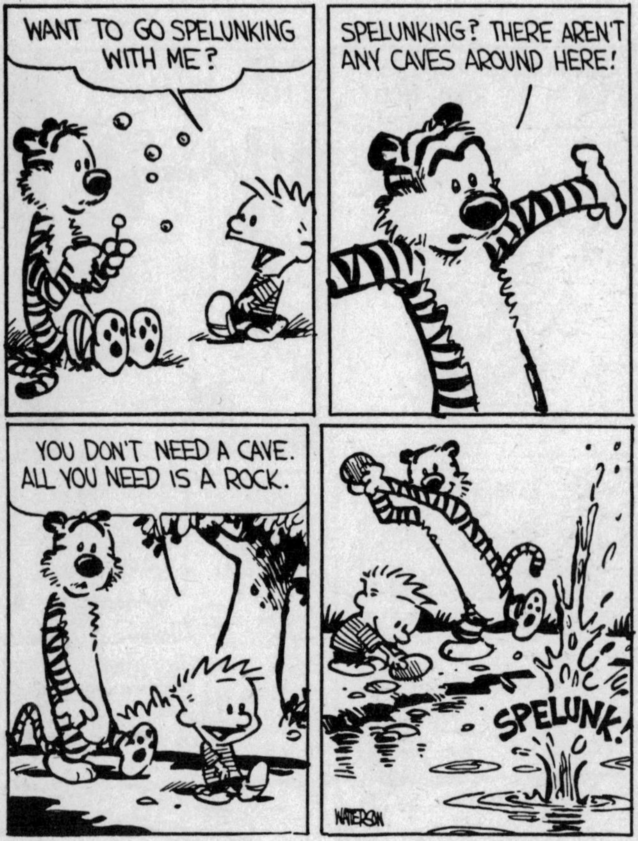
WANT TO GO SPELUNKING WITH ME?
SPELUNKING? THERE AREN'T ANY CAVES AROUND HERE!
YOU DON'T NEED A CAVE. ALL YOU NEED IS A ROCK.
SPELUNK!
WATERSON

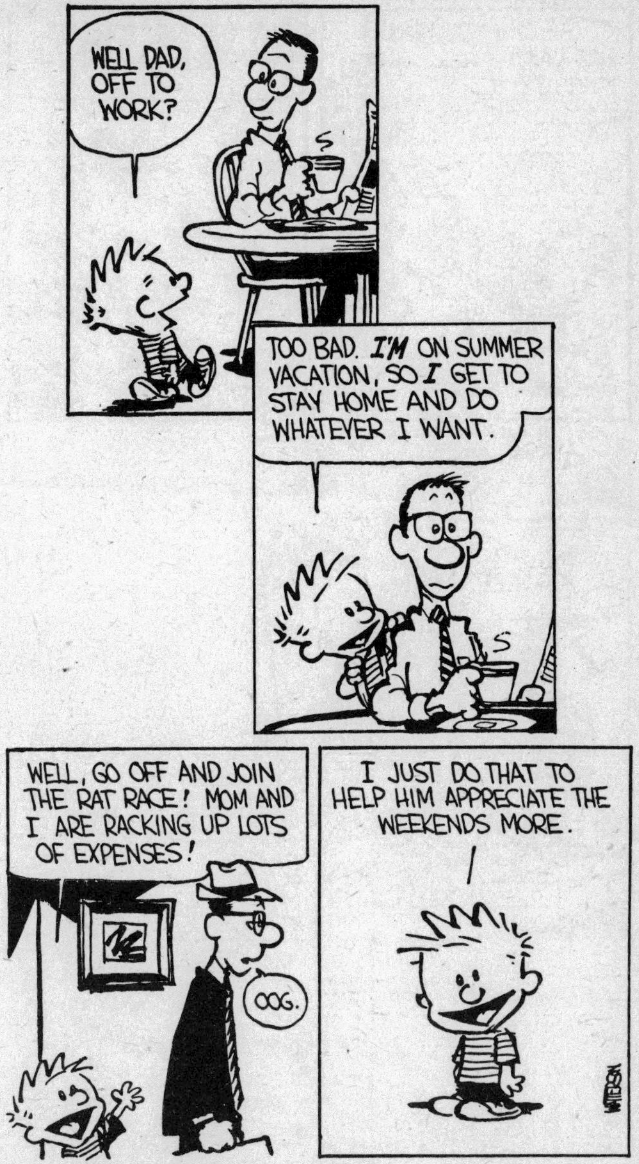
WELL DAD, OFF TO WORK?
TOO BAD. *I'M* ON SUMMER VACATION, SO *I* GET TO STAY HOME AND DO WHATEVER I WANT.
WELL, GO OFF AND JOIN THE RAT RACE! MOM AND I ARE RACKING UP LOTS OF EXPENSES!
OOG.
I JUST DO THAT TO HELP HIM APPRECIATE THE WEEKENDS MORE.
WATTERSON

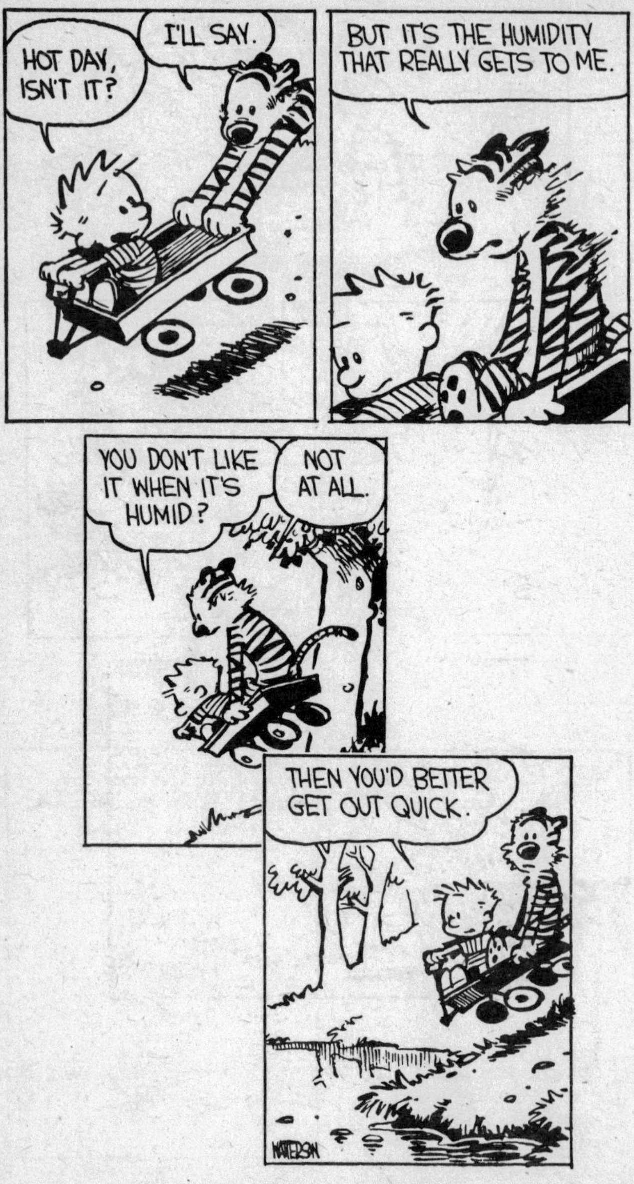
HOT DAY, ISN'T IT?
I'LL SAY.
BUT IT'S THE HUMIDITY THAT REALLY GETS TO ME.
YOU DON'T LIKE IT WHEN IT'S HUMID?
NOT AT ALL.
THEN YOU'D BETTER GET OUT QUICK.
WATTERSON

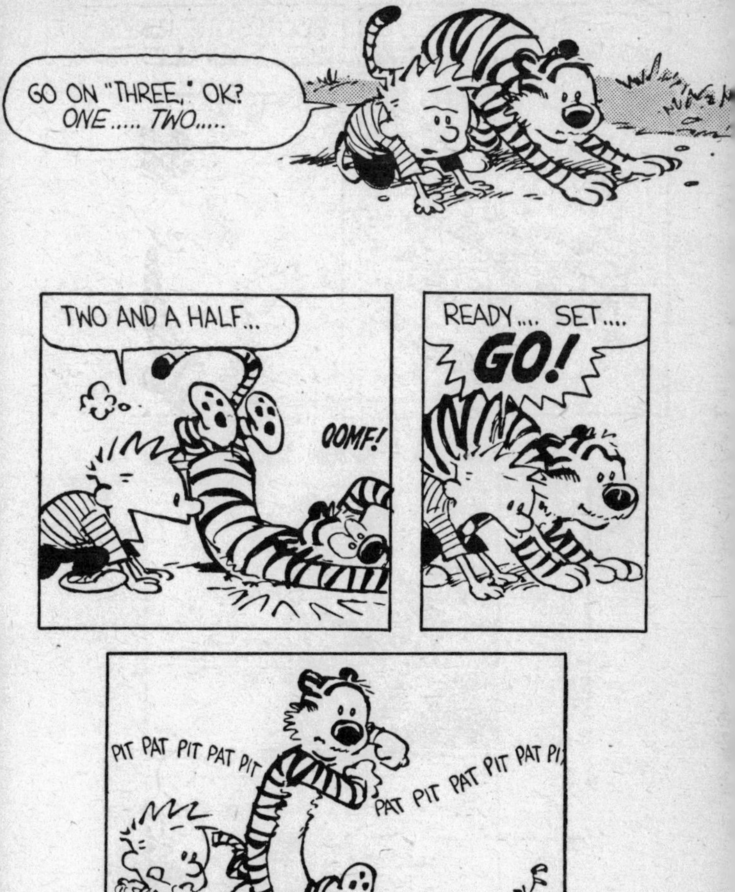
GO ON "THREE," OK? ONE..... TWO.....
TWO AND A HALF...
OOMF!
READY.... SET....
GO!
PIT PAT PIT PAT PIT
PAT PIT PAT PIT PAT PI

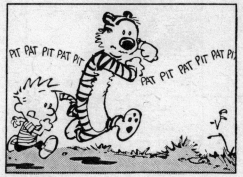

PITTIDA DITTIDA PITTIDA DITTIDA PITTI
CHOOGA CHOOGA CHOOGA CHOO

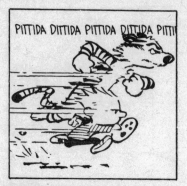

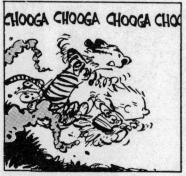

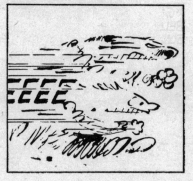

NYEEOWWW
*GASP* I CAN'T BELIEVE IT! NO SONIC BOOM! NOT EVEN A "POP"!
I HEARD A POP, BUT I THINK IT WAS MY LUNGS.
WATTERSON

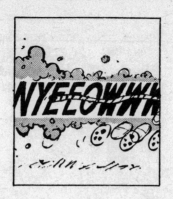

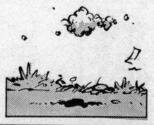

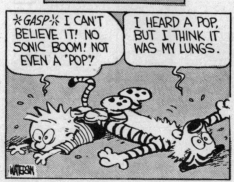

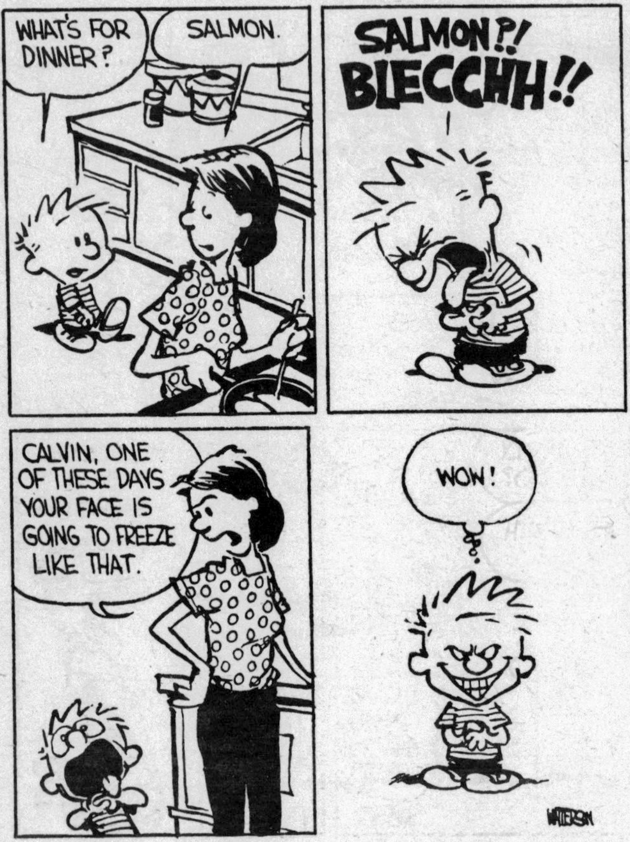
WHAT'S FOR DINNER?
SALMON.
SALMON?! BLECCHH!!
CALVIN, ONE OF THESE DAYS YOUR FACE IS GOING TO FREEZE LIKE THAT.
WOW!
WATTERSON

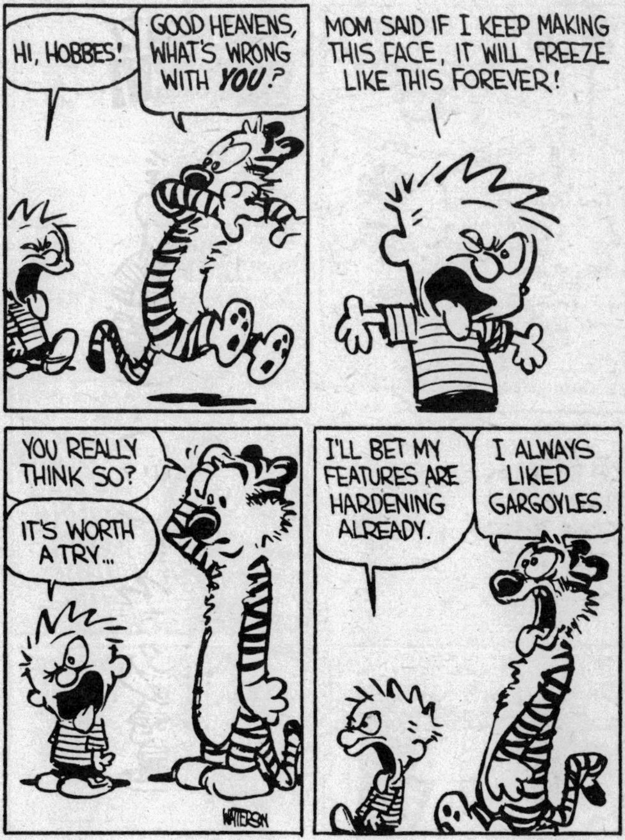
HI, HOBBES!
GOOD HEAVENS, WHAT'S WRONG WITH YOU?
MOM SAID IF I KEEP MAKING THIS FACE, IT WILL FREEZE LIKE THIS FOREVER!
YOU REALLY THINK SO?
IT'S WORTH A TRY...
I'LL BET MY FEATURES ARE HARDENING ALREADY.
I ALWAYS LIKED GARGOYLES.
WATTERSON

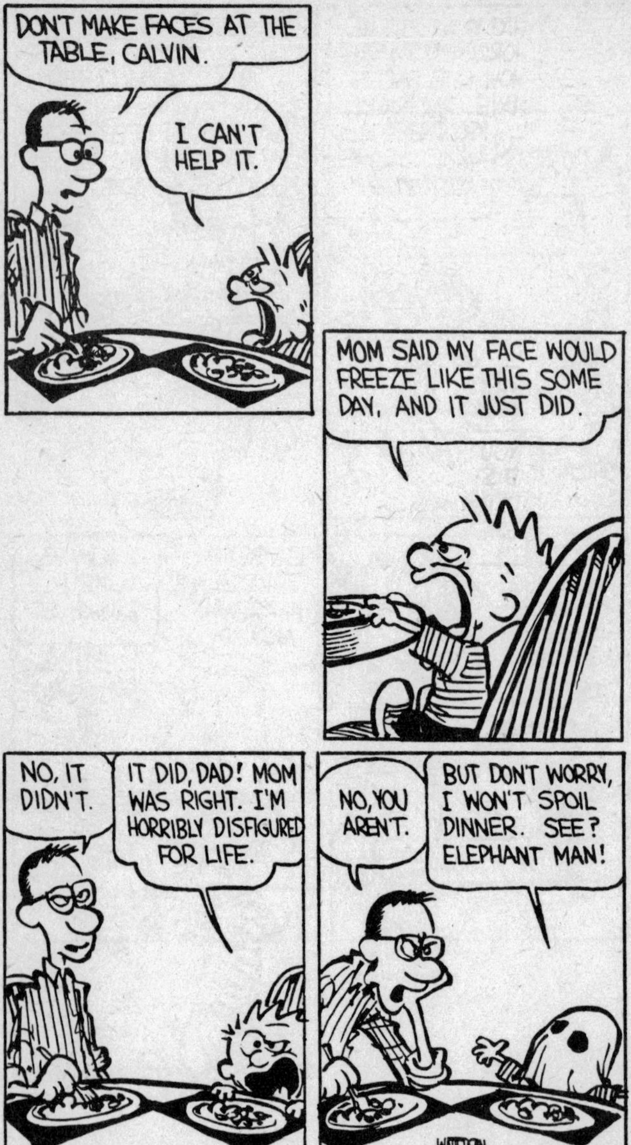
DON'T MAKE FACES AT THE TABLE, CALVIN.
I CAN'T HELP IT.
MOM SAID MY FACE WOULD FREEZE LIKE THIS SOME DAY, AND IT JUST DID.
NO, IT DIDN'T.
IT DID, DAD! MOM WAS RIGHT. I'M HORRIBLY DISFIGURED FOR LIFE.
NO, YOU AREN'T.
BUT DON'T WORRY, I WON'T SPOIL DINNER. SEE? ELEPHANT MAN!
WATTERSON

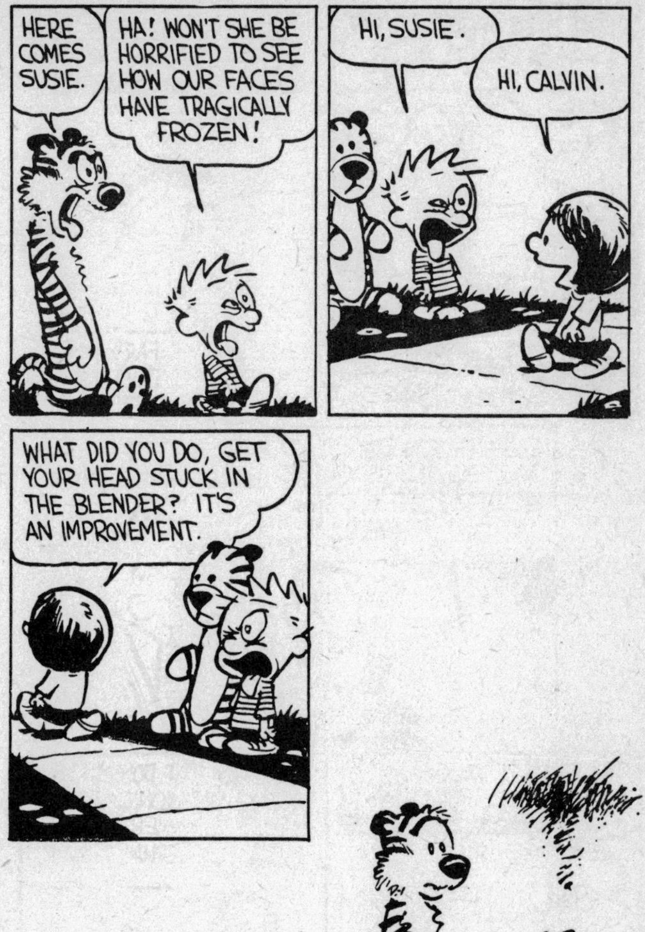
HERE COMES SUSIE.
HA! WON'T SHE BE HORRIFIED TO SEE HOW OUR FACES HAVE TRAGICALLY FROZEN!
HI, SUSIE.
HI, CALVIN.
WHAT DID YOU DO, GET YOUR HEAD STUCK IN THE BLENDER? IT'S AN IMPROVEMENT.
WATTERSON

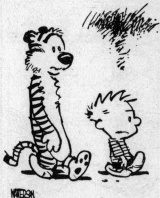

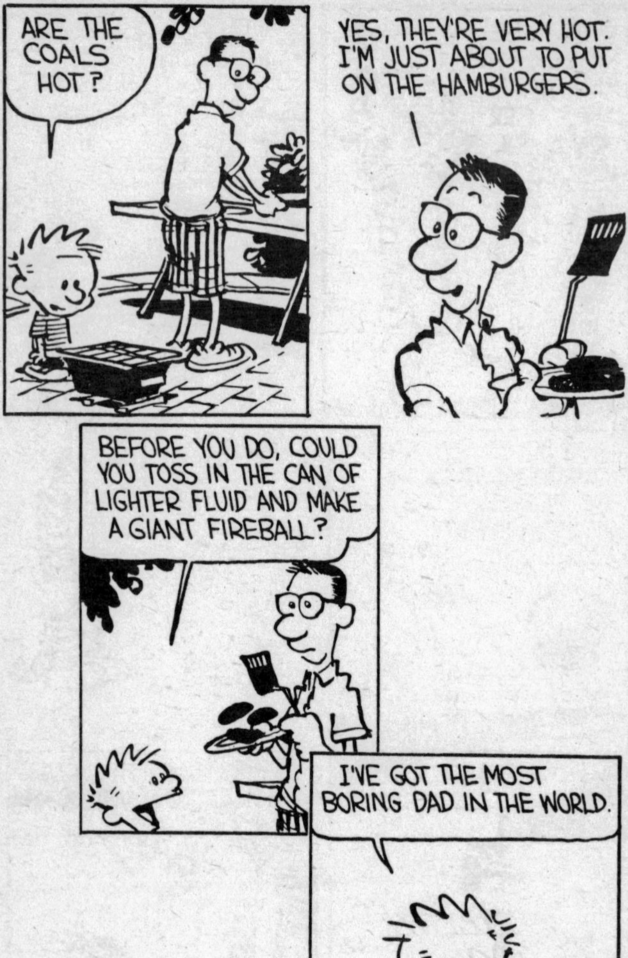
ARE THE COALS HOT?
YES, THEY'RE VERY HOT. I'M JUST ABOUT TO PUT ON THE HAMBURGERS.
BEFORE YOU DO, COULD YOU TOSS IN THE CAN OF LIGHTER FLUID AND MAKE A GIANT FIREBALL?
I'VE GOT THE MOST BORING DAD IN THE WORLD.

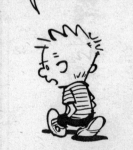

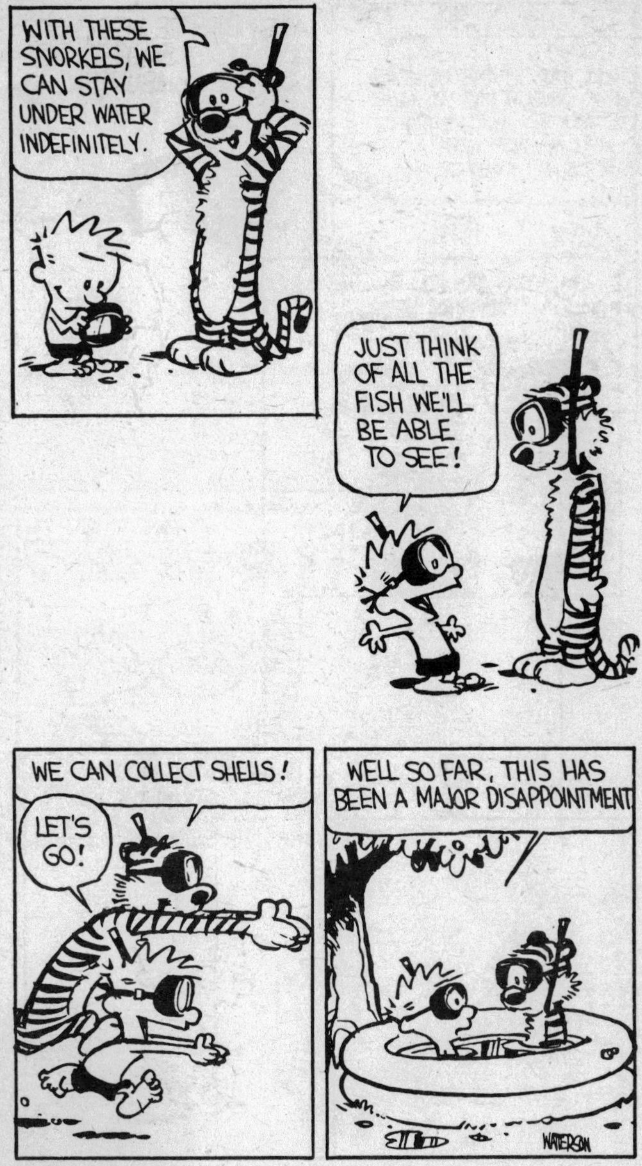
WITH THESE SNORKELS, WE CAN STAY UNDER WATER INDEFINITELY.
JUST THINK OF ALL THE FISH WE'LL BE ABLE TO SEE!
WE CAN COLLECT SHELLS!
LET'S GO!
WELL SO FAR, THIS HAS BEEN A MAJOR DISAPPOINTMENT.
WATERSON

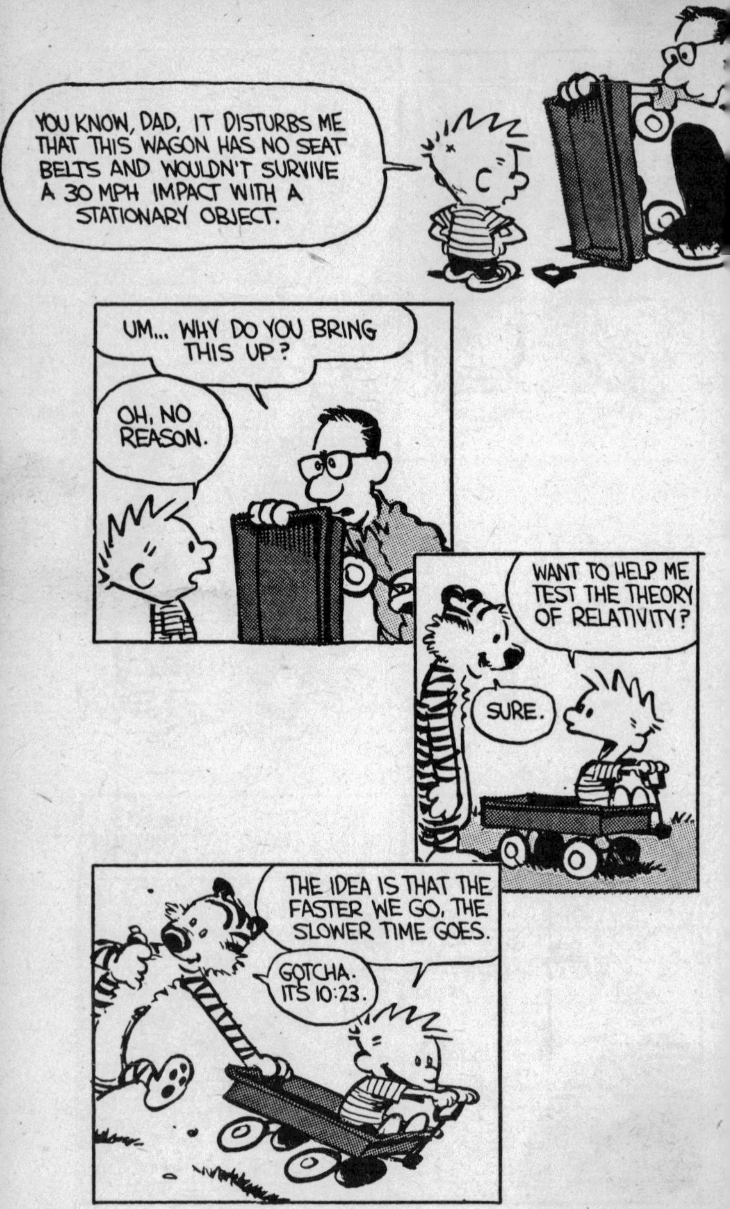

YOU KNOW, DAD, IT DISTURBS ME THAT THIS WAGON HAS NO SEAT BELTS AND WOULDN'T SURVIVE A 30 MPH IMPACT WITH A STATIONARY OBJECT.
UM... WHY DO YOU BRING THIS UP?
OH, NO REASON.
WANT TO HELP ME TEST THE THEORY OF RELATIVITY?
SURE.
THE IDEA IS THAT THE FASTER WE GO, THE SLOWER TIME GOES.
GOTCHA. IT'S 10:23.

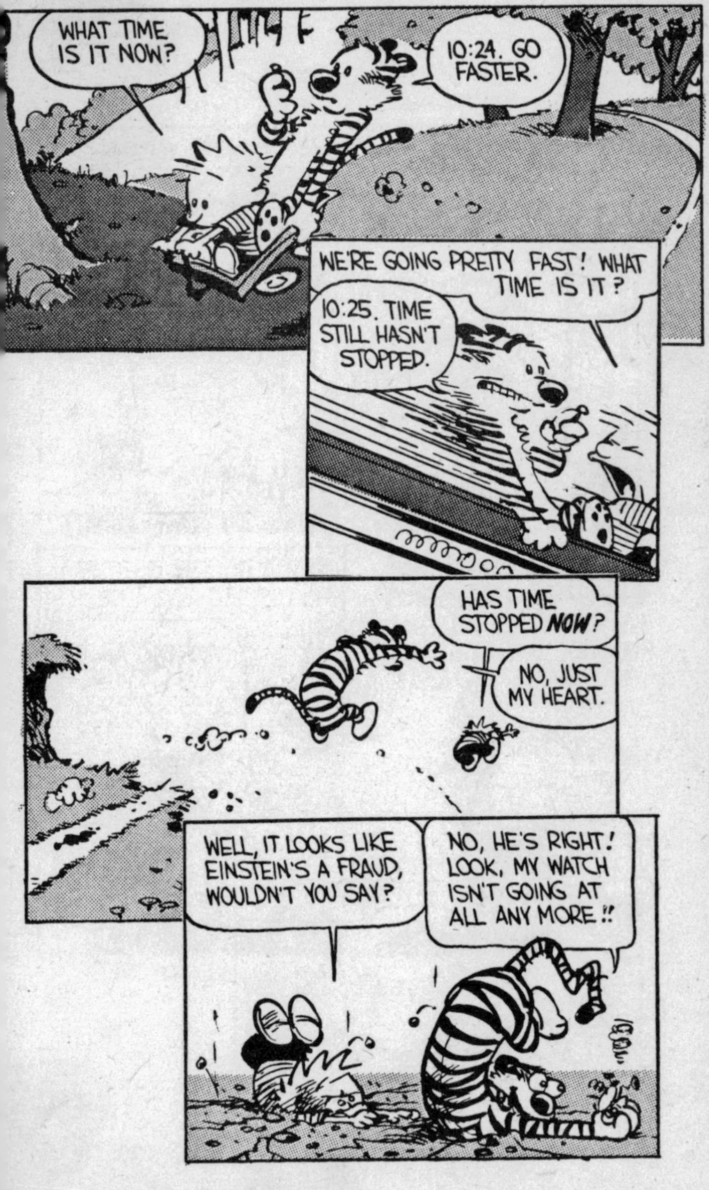
WHAT TIME IS IT NOW?
10:24. GO FASTER.
WE'RE GOING PRETTY FAST! WHAT TIME IS IT?
10:25. TIME STILL HASN'T STOPPED.
HAS TIME STOPPED NOW?
NO, JUST MY HEART.
WELL, IT LOOKS LIKE EINSTEIN'S A FRAUD, WOULDN'T YOU SAY?
NO, HE'S RIGHT! LOOK, MY WATCH ISN'T GOING AT ALL ANY MORE!!

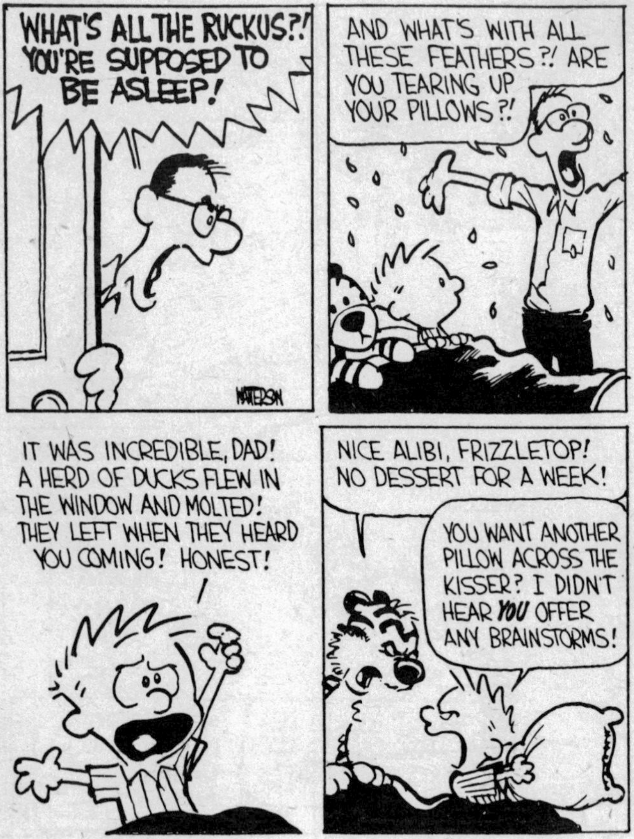
WHAT'S ALL THE RUCKUS?! YOU'RE SUPPOSED TO BE ASLEEP!
WATERSON
AND WHAT'S WITH ALL THESE FEATHERS?! ARE YOU TEARING UP YOUR PILLOWS?!
IT WAS INCREDIBLE, DAD! A HERD OF DUCKS FLEW IN THE WINDOW AND MOLTED! THEY LEFT WHEN THEY HEARD YOU COMING! HONEST!
NICE ALIBI, FRIZZLETOP! NO DESSERT FOR A WEEK!
YOU WANT ANOTHER PILLOW ACROSS THE KISSER? I DIDN'T HEAR **YOU** OFFER ANY BRAINSTORMS!

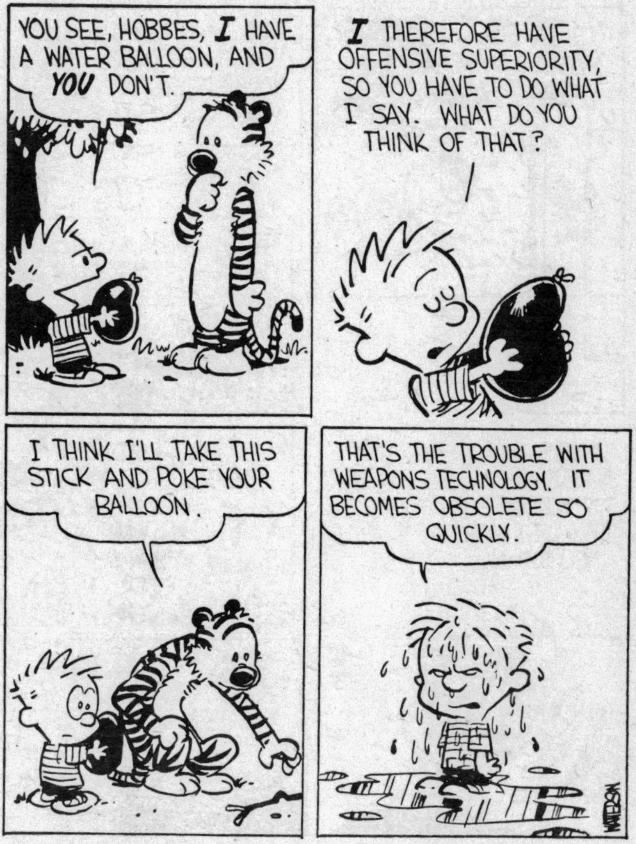
YOU SEE, HOBBES, I HAVE A WATER BALLOON, AND YOU DON'T.
I THEREFORE HAVE OFFENSIVE SUPERIORITY, SO YOU HAVE TO DO WHAT I SAY. WHAT DO YOU THINK OF THAT?
I THINK I'LL TAKE THIS STICK AND POKE YOUR BALLOON.
THAT'S THE TROUBLE WITH WEAPONS TECHNOLOGY. IT BECOMES OBSOLETE SO QUICKLY.
WATTERSON

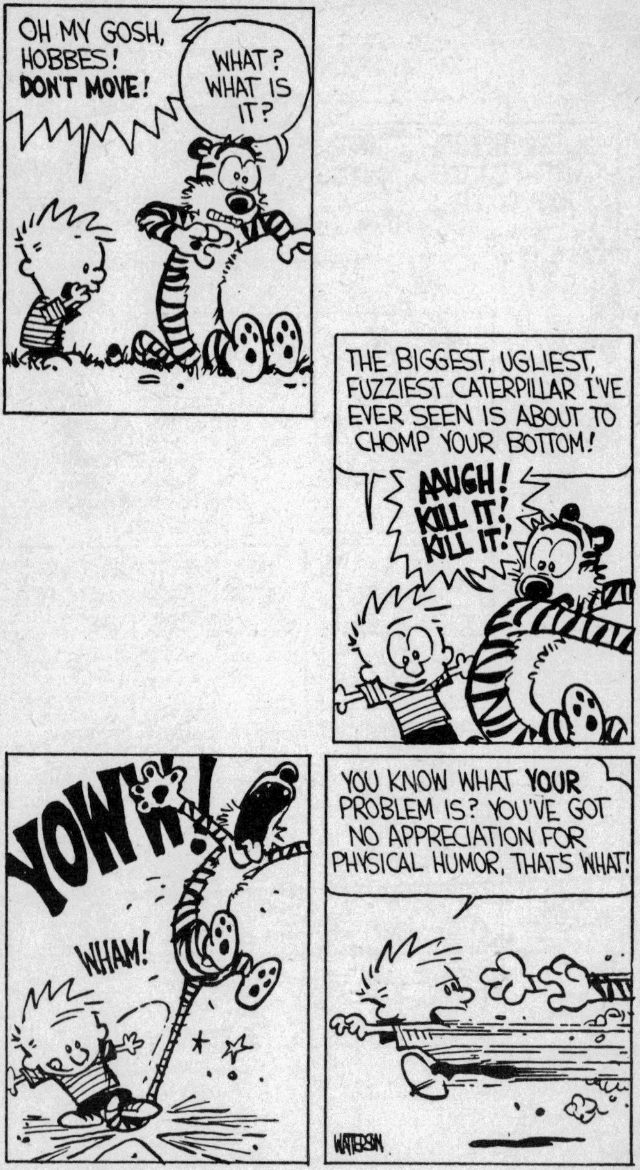
OH MY GOSH, HOBBES! DON'T MOVE!
WHAT? WHAT IS IT?
THE BIGGEST, UGLIEST, FUZZIEST CATERPILLAR I'VE EVER SEEN IS ABOUT TO CHOMP YOUR BOTTOM!
AAUGH! KILL IT! KILL IT!
YOWW!
WHAM!
YOU KNOW WHAT YOUR PROBLEM IS? YOU'VE GOT NO APPRECIATION FOR PHYSICAL HUMOR, THAT'S WHAT!
WATTERSON

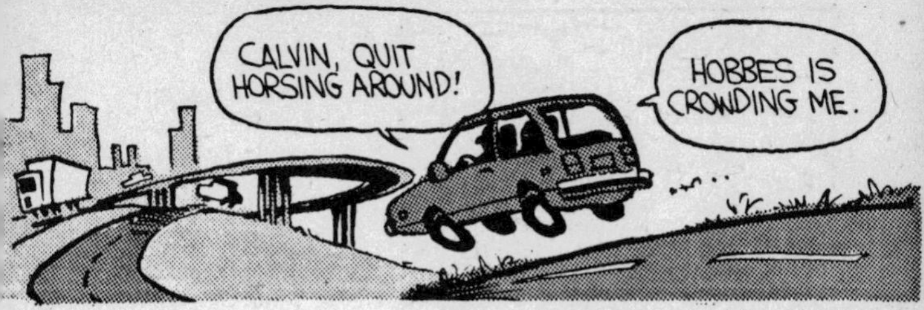
CALVIN, QUIT HORSING AROUND!
HOBBES IS CROWDING ME.

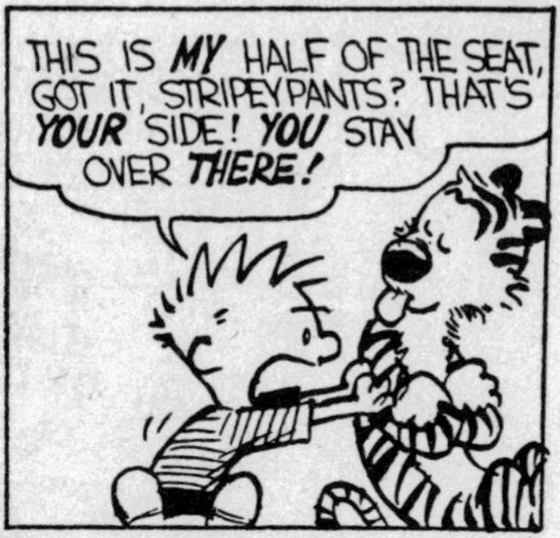
THIS IS MY HALF OF THE SEAT, GOT IT, STRIPEYPANTS? THAT'S YOUR SIDE! YOU STAY OVER THERE!

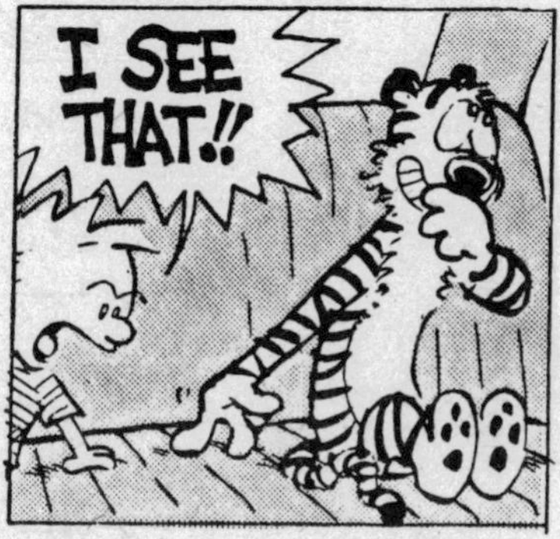
I SEE THAT!!

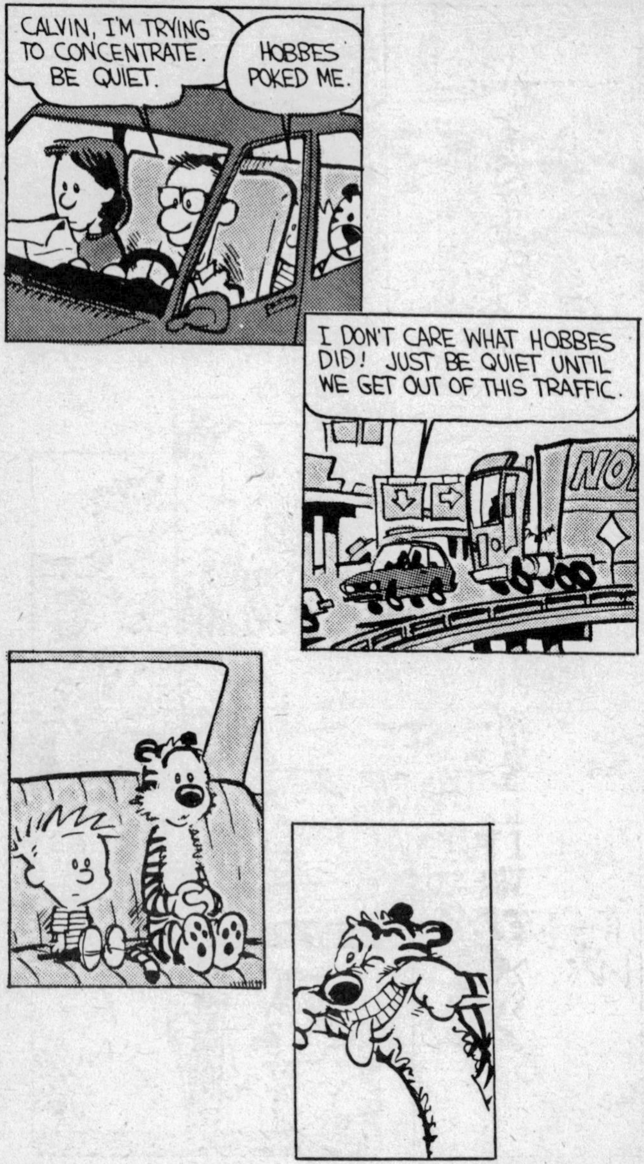
CALVIN, I'M TRYING TO CONCENTRATE. BE QUIET.
HOBBES POKED ME.
I DON'T CARE WHAT HOBBES DID! JUST BE QUIET UNTIL WE GET OUT OF THIS TRAFFIC.

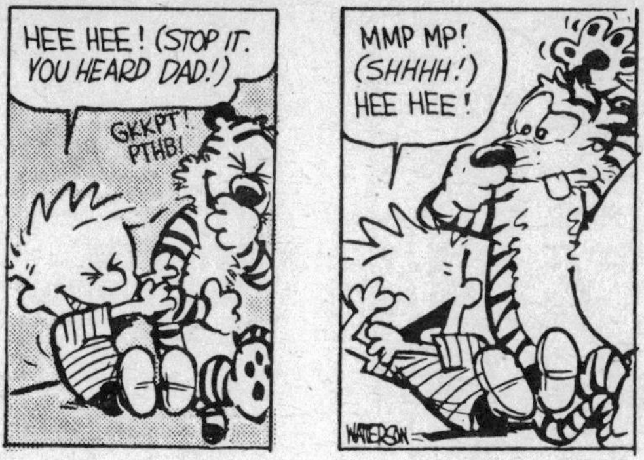
HEE HEE! (STOP IT. YOU HEARD DAD!)
GKKPT! PTHB!
MMP MP! (SHHHH!) HEE HEE!
WATTERSON

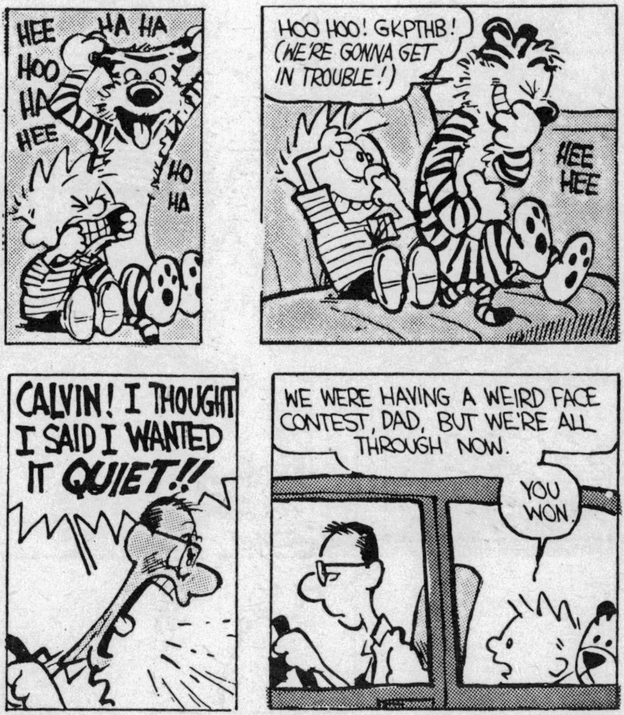
HEE HOO HA HEE
HA HA
HO HA
HOO HOO! GKPTHB! (WE'RE GONNA GET IN TROUBLE!)
HEE HEE
CALVIN! I THOUGHT I SAID I WANTED IT QUIET!!
WE WERE HAVING A WEIRD FACE CONTEST, DAD, BUT WE'RE ALL THROUGH NOW.
YOU WON.

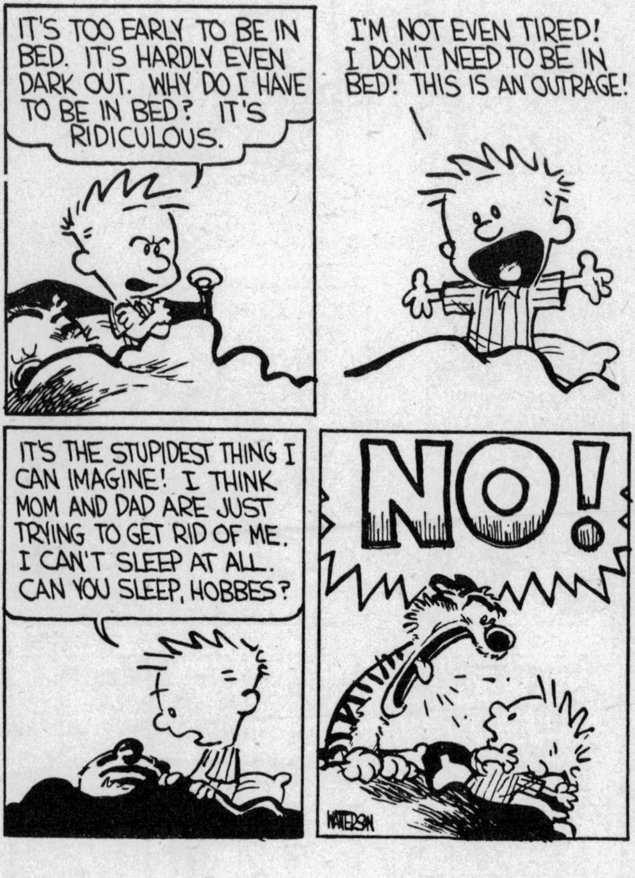
IT'S TOO EARLY TO BE IN BED. IT'S HARDLY EVEN DARK OUT. WHY DO I HAVE TO BE IN BED? IT'S RIDICULOUS.
I'M NOT EVEN TIRED! I DON'T NEED TO BE IN BED! THIS IS AN OUTRAGE!
IT'S THE STUPIDEST THING I CAN IMAGINE! I THINK MOM AND DAD ARE JUST TRYING TO GET RID OF ME. I CAN'T SLEEP AT ALL. CAN YOU SLEEP, HOBBES?
NO!
WATTERSON

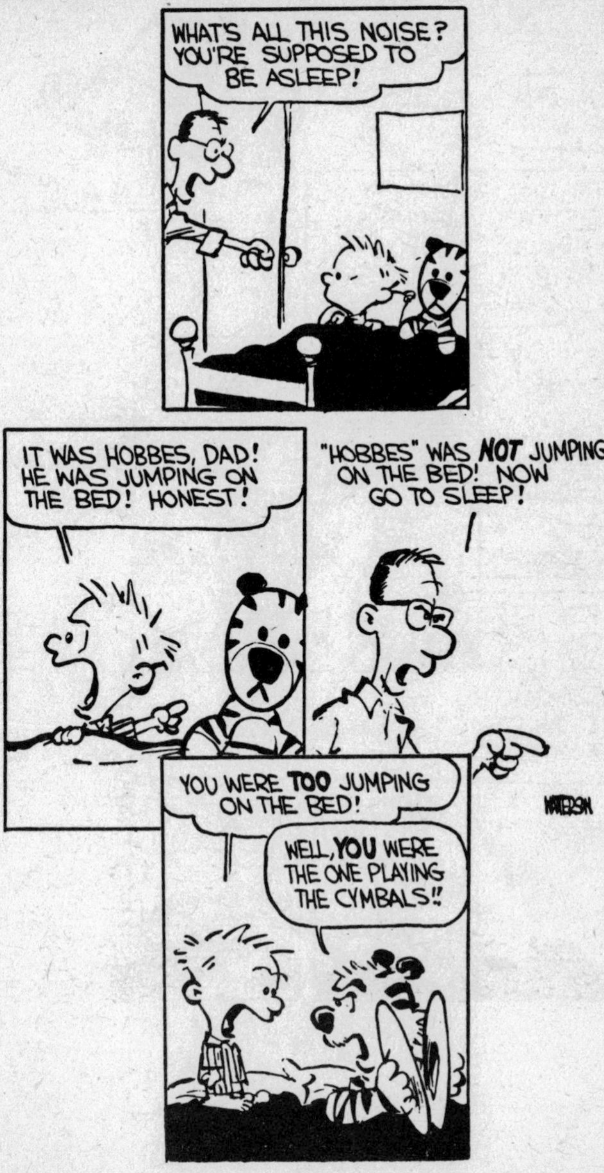
WHAT'S ALL THIS NOISE? YOU'RE SUPPOSED TO BE ASLEEP!
IT WAS HOBBES, DAD! HE WAS JUMPING ON THE BED! HONEST!
"HOBBES" WAS NOT JUMPING ON THE BED! NOW GO TO SLEEP!
YOU WERE TOO JUMPING ON THE BED!
WELL, YOU WERE THE ONE PLAYING THE CYMBALS!!
WATERSON

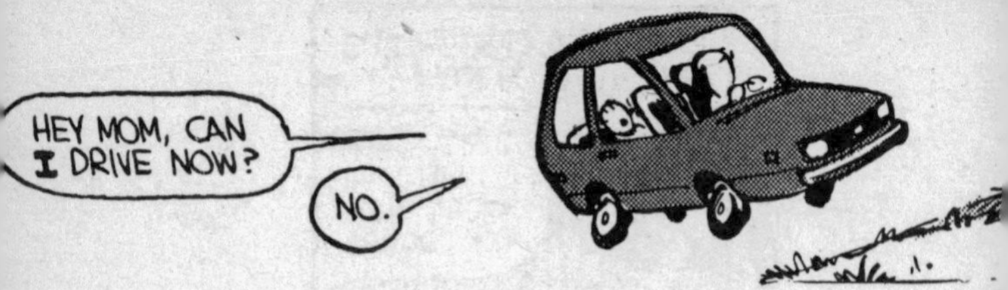
HEY MOM, CAN I DRIVE NOW?
NO.

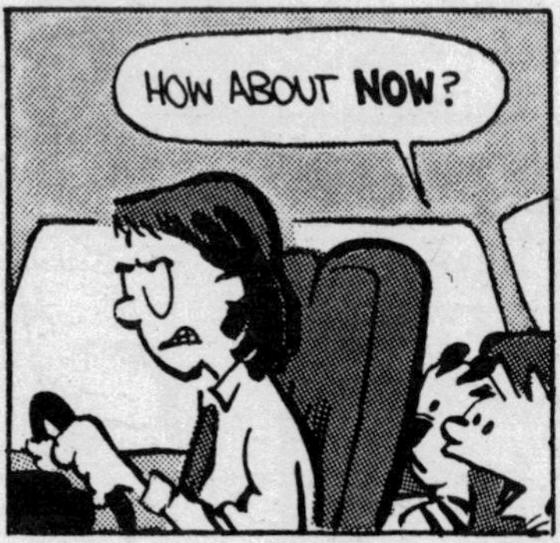
HOW ABOUT NOW?

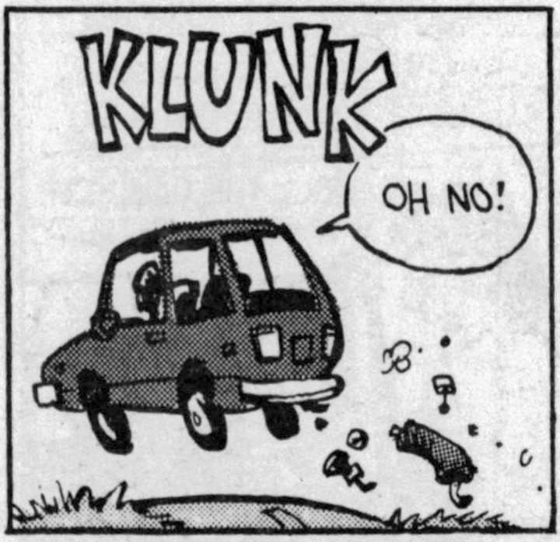
KLUNK
OH NO!

OH YOU STUPID CAR! WHAT'S WRONG WITH YOU NOW?!?
THAT'S IT, MOM! GO AHEAD AND SWEAR! WE DON'T MIND!
CALVIN, BE QUIET!
WANT HOBBES AND ME TO GO GET HELP?
YOU STAY WHERE YOU ARE. I'LL LOOK UNDER THE HOOD.
KICK THE CAR, MOM! IT WORKS ON THE TV!

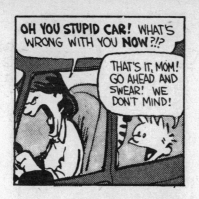

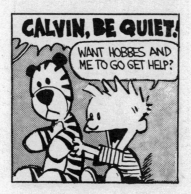

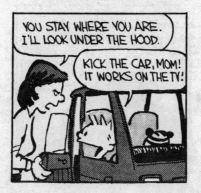

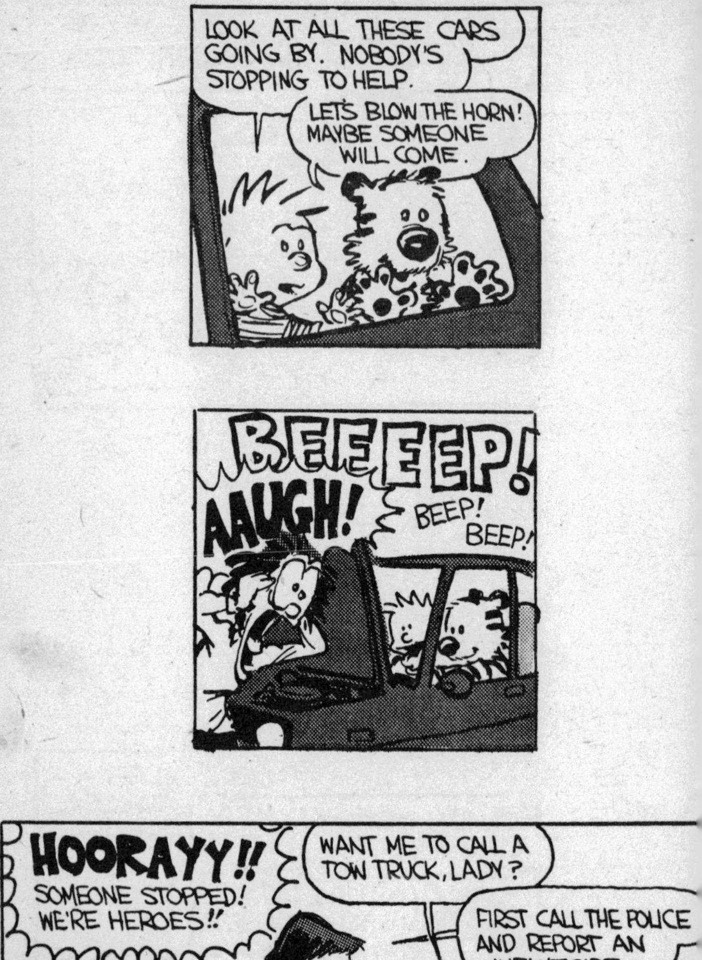

LOOK AT ALL THESE CARS GOING BY. NOBODY'S STOPPING TO HELP.
LET'S BLOW THE HORN! MAYBE SOMEONE WILL COME.
BEEEEP!
AAUGH!
BEEP! BEEP!
HOORAYY!! SOMEONE STOPPED! WE'RE HEROES!!
WANT ME TO CALL A TOW TRUCK, LADY?
FIRST CALL THE POLICE AND REPORT AN INFANTICIDE.
WATTERSON

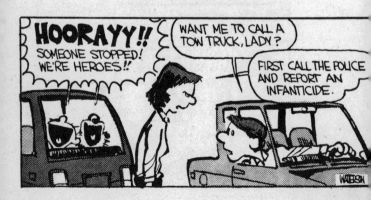

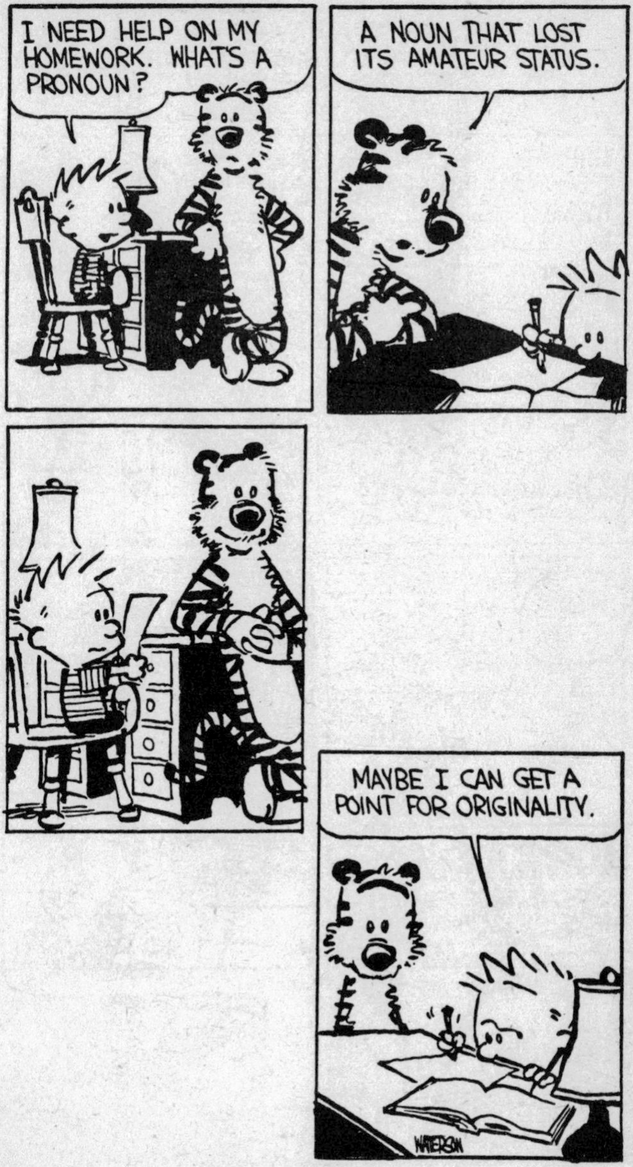
I NEED HELP ON MY HOMEWORK. WHAT'S A PRONOUN?
A NOUN THAT LOST ITS AMATEUR STATUS.
MAYBE I CAN GET A POINT FOR ORIGINALITY.
WATTERSON

HOBBES, WHAT SHOULD I DO WHEN MOE COMES TO BEAT ME UP IN GYM CLASS?
WELL, YOU CAN ALWAYS DO WHAT WE TIGERS DO WHEN A RHINO CHARGES.
WATERSON
WHAT'S THAT?
WE SCRAMBLE LIKE MANIACS FOR THE NEAREST TREE.
THAT'S YOUR ADVICE?? TO SIT IN A TREE ALL DAY?!?
IT DOESN'T IMPRESS THE GIRLS, OF COURSE, BUT THERE'S NO SENSE IMPRESSING THEM AND THEN GETTING KILLED, MY DAD USED TO SAY...

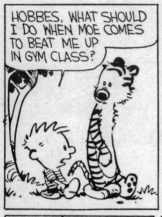

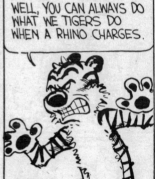

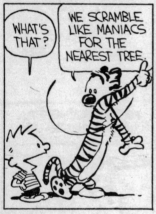

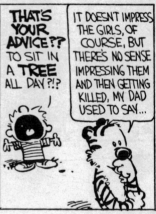

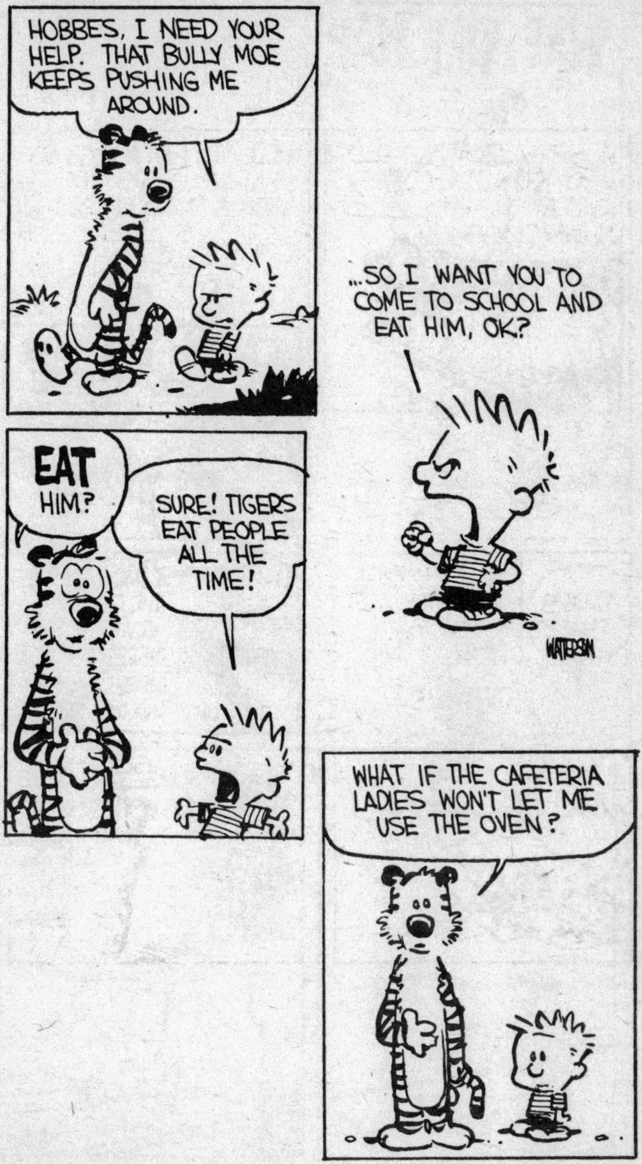
HOBBES, I NEED YOUR HELP. THAT BULLY MOE KEEPS PUSHING ME AROUND.
...SO I WANT YOU TO COME TO SCHOOL AND EAT HIM, OK?
WATTERSON
EAT HIM?
SURE! TIGERS EAT PEOPLE ALL THE TIME!
WHAT IF THE CAFETERIA LADIES WON'T LET ME USE THE OVEN?

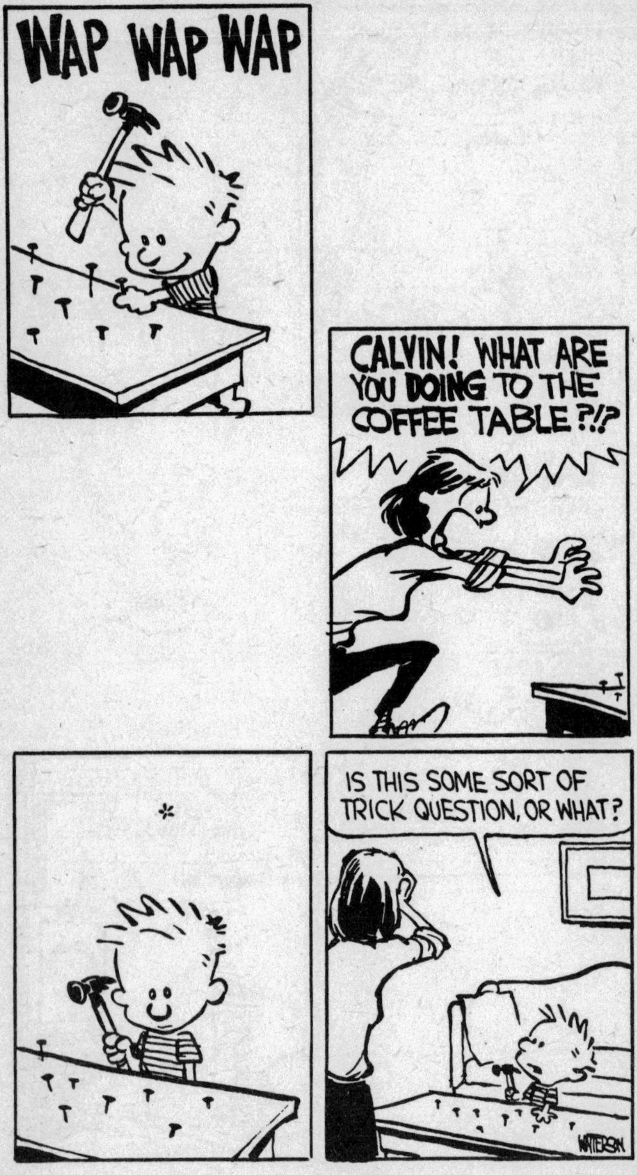
WAP WAP WAP
CALVIN! WHAT ARE YOU DOING TO THE COFFEE TABLE?!?
IS THIS SOME SORT OF TRICK QUESTION, OR WHAT?
WATTERSON

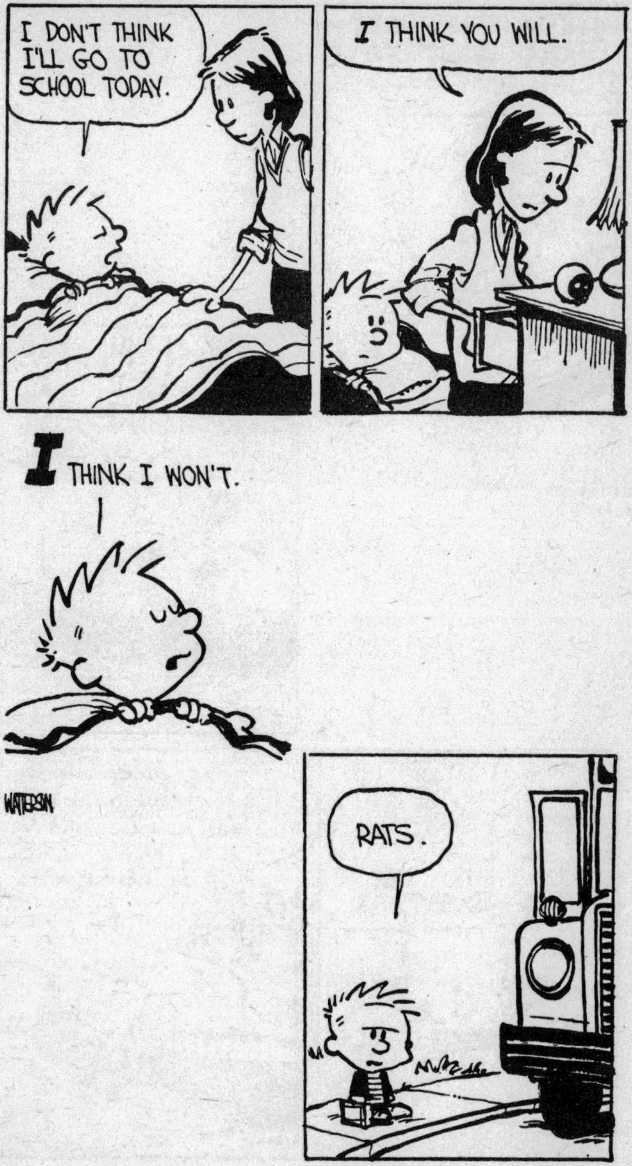
I DON'T THINK I'LL GO TO SCHOOL TODAY.
I THINK YOU WILL.
I THINK I WON'T.
WATTERSON
RATS.

WOW, LOOK DOWN THERE! I THINK THAT'S THE DIM OUTLINE OF A WHALE!
I THINK THAT'S A ROCK.
AND THAT MUST BE A GIANT EEL SLITHERING UP FROM THE BOTTOM!
WATTERSON
I THINK THAT'S A WEED.
I'LL BET THIS IS THE MAST OF AN OLD SPANISH GALLEON, SUNK HUNDREDS OF YEARS AGO.
IT'S A BRANCH.
*MAN*, THIS IS BORING. I WISH THERE WAS A MOVIE THEATER SOMEPLACE.

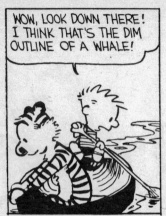

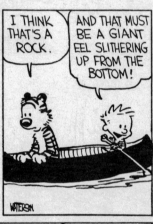

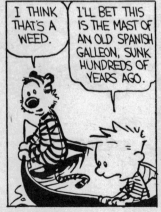

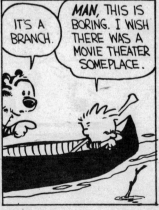

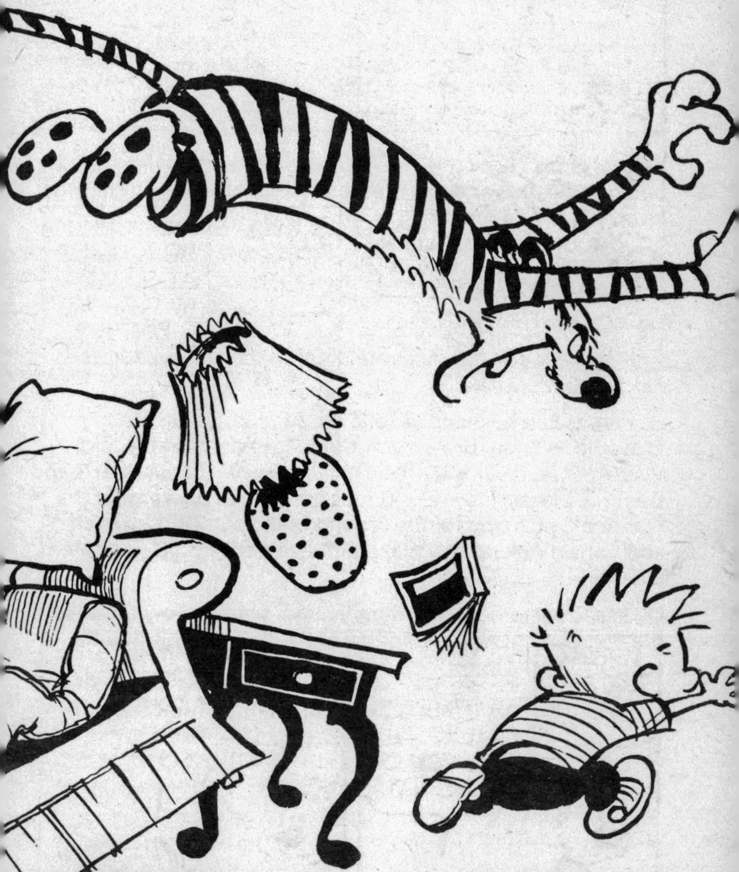

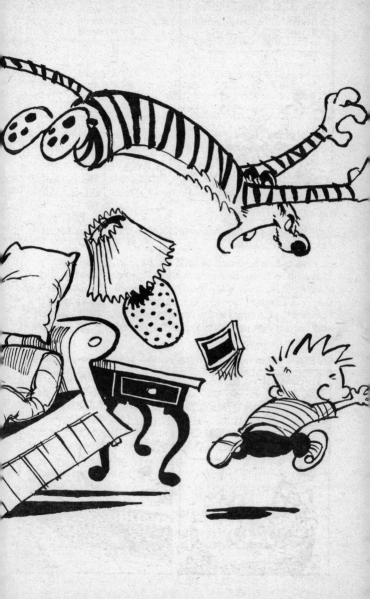

| | | | |
|---|---|---|---|
| ☐ | Calvin and Hobbes Vol 1 | Bill Watterson | £3.50 |
| ☐ | Calvin and Hobbes Vol 2 | Bill Watterson | £3.50 |
| ☐ | Something Under the Bed is Drooling | Bill Watterson | £5.99 |
| ☐ | Yukon Ho! | Bill Watterson | £5.99 |
| ☐ | Weirdos From Another Planet | Bill Watterson | £5.99 |
| ☐ | Lazy Sunday Book | Bill Watterson | £6.99 |
| ☐ | Revenge of the Baby-Sat | Bill Watterson | £5.99 |
| ☐ | Authoritative Calvin and Hobbes | Bill Watterson | £7.99 |
| ☐ | Scientific Progress Goes 'Boink' | Bill Watterson | £5.99 |
| ☐ | Attack of the Deranged Mutant Killer Monster Snow Goons | Bill Watterson | £5.99 |

Warner Books now offers an exciting range of quality titles by both established and new authors. All of the books in this the series are available from:
   Little, Brown and Company (UK),
   P.O. Box 11,
   Falmouth,
   Cornwall TR10 9EN.

Alternatively you may fax your order to the above address.
Fax No. 0326 376423.

Payments can be made as follows: cheque, postal order (payable to Little, Brown and Company) or by credit cards, Visa/Access. Do not send cash or currency. UK customers and B.F.P.O. please allow £1.00 for postage and packing for the first book, plus 50p for the second book, plus 30p for each additional book up to a maximum charge of £3.00 (7 books plus).

Overseas customers including Ireland, please allow £2.00 for the first book plus £1.00 for the second book, plus 50p for each additional book.

NAME (Block Letters) ..............................................................

..............................................................................................

ADDRESS .............................................................................

..............................................................................................

..............................................................................................

☐ I enclose my remittance for ................................................

☐ I wish to pay by Access/Visa Card

Number ☐☐☐☐☐☐☐☐☐☐☐☐☐☐☐☐☐☐☐

Card Expiry Date ☐☐☐☐